SUSAN SARGENT'S
New Country Color

THE ART OF LIVING

SUSAN SARGENT'S
New Country Color

THE ART OF LIVING

Susan Sargent
and Jake Chapline

PHOTOGRAPHY BY ERIC ROTH

WATSON-GUPTILL PUBLICATIONS / NEW YORK

First published in 2002 by
Watson-Guptill Publications,
a division of VNU Business Media, Inc.
770 Broadway, New York, N.Y. 10003
www.watsonguptill.com

Library of Congress Cataloging-in-Publication Data

Sargent, Susan.
    New country color : the art of living / Susan Sargent and Jake Chapline ;
major photography by Eric Roth.
       p. cm.
    Includes index.
    ISBN 0-8230-2184-X
    1. Interior decoration—United States—History—20th century. 2. Color in interior
decoration. I. Chapline, Jake. II. Title.
    NK2004 .S27 2002
    747' .94—dc21

                                                                2001007726

Senior Acquisitions Editor: Victoria Craven
Senior Editor: Julie Mazur
Designer: Areta Buk
Production Manager: Ellen Greene
The principal typeface used in the composition of this book was 10.75-point Adobe Caslon

Printed in the USA

First printing, 2002

1 2 3 4 5 6 7 8 / 09 08 07 06 05 04 03 02

TO MY MOTHER, JOAN SARGENT,

AND THE MANY COLORS OF HER GARDEN,

AND TO MY HUSBAND, TOM PETERS,

FOR HIS UNBOUNDED ENTHUSIASMS

Contents

Preface: Beginnings 8

Acknowledgments 11

✻

Dream, Design,
Decorate 12

✻

Entryways, Halls, and
Stairways 34

Kitchens 48

Dining Rooms 64

Living Rooms 78

Bedrooms 96

Bathrooms 116

Outdoor Spaces 130

✻

Pulling It All Together:
The Grover Farm 144

✻

Source Directory 159

Index 160

Beginnings

About a year ago, I sat down at my kitchen table with a pot of tea, a blank pad of paper, and a draft outline of the material I wanted to cover in this book. I had been thinking about the book for a long time, and as it was a raw, rainy April day, I was looking forward to spending the afternoon jotting down ideas about decorating for the benefit of an appreciative posterity.

Several hours later, the tea was cold, my legs were cramped from sitting too long, and the pad of paper in front of me was blank except for a tangle of doodles. The rain had stopped and it looked like the sun might come out, so I abandoned the work I had planned to do and went out with my three dogs to look for signs of spring in the field above my house. When I came back to the book days later, I was exactly where I had been before: full of ideas, with no clue where to start.

Decorating and writing have two important things in common. First, you put a lot of yourself into both activities, often discovering things about yourself in the process. Everything you've seen and experienced, all of your likes and dislikes, your hopes and expectations, your dreams and sense of humor, become part of your design. The result says something about who you are and may influence who you will become.

Writing and decorating are also both essentially unbounded endeavors. You could start anywhere, throw anything into the mix, and probably make it work, but who knows how what you've done might affect every subsequent choice? You might write a sentence about the taste of a madeleine and, like Proust, not stop for three thousand pages. Or you might select new fabric for an armchair and discover five years later that you've completely redecorated (or even remodeled) your home. You just never know the end at the beginning, which makes beginning at all seem kind of reckless.

For me, curiosity and the appeal of getting paint all over myself are much stronger than any anxiety about how things will turn out. I really want to see where a different color on the bedroom walls or a hand-painted design on the floor of the sun porch might take me. Besides, I know from experience that if a decorating idea doesn't work out, it won't go so wrong that I can't fix it.

Spaces, especially interior spaces, have a lot to do with who we are and how we feel about the world and ourselves. That's one reason why I think it's important to take a direct hand in creating a home that reflects your own taste and personality. Another reason is because it's fun and exciting to make the things you see and use every day more beautiful for yourself and the people around you. The purpose of this book is to encourage and help you to do just that. It expresses my interior-decorating philosophy, developed over twenty-five years as an artist and artisan creating decorative home furnishings. It's about things that you—you yourself, not a professional designer or decorator—can do to make dramatic changes in the way your home looks and feels.

"IF I WERE ASKED TO NAME THE CHIEF BENEFIT OF THE HOUSE, I SHOULD SAY THE HOUSE SHELTERS DAYDREAMING, THE HOUSE PROTECTS THE DREAMER, THE HOUSE ALLOWS ONE TO DREAM IN PEACE."

Gaston Bachelard, philosopher and poet, 1884–1962

Exuberant colors and free-hand designs are characteristic of my approach to decoration. I painted this wall in my younger son's bedroom when he was small. My grandmother gave me the antique child's chair, which has been re-covered in a woven fabric (see "How to Do It: Reupholstered Chairs" on page 72).

My intention is that *New Country Color* will serve as a counterpoint to the bland and costly interior-design model so prevalent today. Excessive concern about good taste and over reliance on the packaged "look" of particular decorators and home furnishings manufacturers have caused an epidemic of sameness in American homes. Too many people read the popular house magazines, buy all of the "right" materials and furnishings (generally safe and coordinated) and then discover that their home lacks a personality of its own.

I hope to show you how to make your rooms more interesting, personal, and vivid through the casual use of paint and pattern. Above all, I will encourage you to experiment. Being creative with your home requires taking chances, expressing yourself, and staying relaxed enough to push on and see how things turn out. Think of it as play, throw yourself into it, don't be afraid of mistakes. What you *won't* find here are hard-and-fast rules for decorating. I will cover some basic principles and suggest ways you can apply them, but my primary purpose is to help you develop and express your own sense of style. I will show you some of the rooms I have created and suggest a number of specific projects that you can do to create the effects you want.

Most of those projects are pretty simple; you can do them in an afternoon or a weekend. That's the essence of decorating to me: not starting with a grand design for redoing a home, but trying out ideas as they occur and as time permits. I love tackling a spur-of-the-moment project, paintbrush in hand and perhaps only the beginning of an idea or the rough form of a pattern in my head. My approach emphasizes spontaneous self-expression and do-it-yourself creativity. I won't tell you how to make your home or your furniture look like someone else's, but how to make them look like your own.

Primarily, this is a book about color. Most people don't realize how powerful and versatile a tool color is. It surrounds us all the time, has a profound effect on our thoughts and emotions, and is infinitely variable. This book is crammed with as many ideas about using color as I could fit. And while I've included other kinds of decorating ideas, too—about finding or making special details; arranging rooms so they work the way you want them to; using fabrics, pillows, and other accents to change the look and feel of a room from season to season—all of them revolve around color.

To a greater extent than I expected, this is also a book about me. I found it difficult to write about my ideas and techniques without discussing where I found them. In addition, as the book came together, I realized more and more that I wanted to share not only information, but also a sense of enthusiasm and excitement, and I didn't think I could do that without revealing something about myself.

Although my work is often classified as "country" style, I am not a proponent of any particular school of design. I live in rural Vermont and find much of my inspiration in the surrounding natural landscape, but I have also lived in cities and in Europe and I believe in an eclectic approach to decoration. I encourage you to take colors, patterns, and objects that delight you and use them in combinations and arrangements that are appealing to you and to others.

Pictures do more than words to express the ideas and sensibilities I want to share, so I have filled this book with photographs of rooms and details to suggest how much you can do with a little paint, patience, and imagination. Most of the photos were taken at the house I live in now, at another house where I lived for many years, and at two houses that were recently renovated to provide office and studio space for my company, Susan Sargent Designs. (I wasn't above doing some on-the-spot decorating with a can of paint and a brush to make a point here and there.) I have also included photos of houses belonging to several Vermont neighbors whose living style—casual, individual, and colorful—reflects their own creativity and love of color.

I had a lot of fun working with photographer Eric Roth to get these pictures. I hope you'll have as much fun looking at them.

Susan Sargent

A flowered wool rug and an antique chair create cheerful splashes of color in this sunny corner of our bedroom. The framed black-and-white photographs, showing scenes of rural England, hang on a distempered violet wall.

Acknowledgments

Projects and houses can evolve over the years, but books and photo shoots have a different reality. I could not have completed this without the hard work of Eric Roth and Jake Chapline, great friends as well as collaborators, who were willing to be infected by my colors and vision. Also, my right hand in the studio, Denise McGinley, who keeps track of my life and will wear multiple hats as needed. Gary Gras was cheerfully available, as always, to shift furniture, and Paul Roberts and crew put up with my eccentricities. Jack Barr, Peter Frank, and Patty O'Shaugnessey gave me great input on making the message cohesive. Thanks also to my neighbors and kindred spirits Randall Perkins, Christine Miles, Carol Colin, and Patty Yoder, for letting us take photographs of their colorful country houses. I am grateful to Andy Pacuk, Barbara Hayes, Gloria Guldberg, Lenwood Rich, Bob Stec, Cindy Petrop-Bailey, Bob Allen, and Nancy Webster for believing in my work. Also to my editor, Victoria Craven, for believing in the story. And finally, in appreciation of my two sons, Max and Ben, who keep me guessing.

A dining room vignette combines an antique embroidered tablecloth and a colorful piece of modern ceramics with one of my favorite colors, the bold yellow of the ranunculus blossom.

Photographer's Note

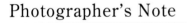

When I first began photographing rooms that were designed by Susan Sargent, I was a bit overwhelmed by her bold color combinations. I was also bemused by her easy, carefree attitude about painting walls, furniture, fabrics—just about anything—with bright colors and designs. I just wasn't used to seeing so much color and exuberance in my own home or in the homes I photograph for books and magazines.

After working with Susan for a few days, however, I began to understand her work. All that color made me feel good. It felt good to be in the rooms, and it felt really good to photograph them. I was having more fun than usual, and the pictures seemed to flow through my camera. I felt confident about allowing them to express the sense of freedom that Susan brings to home decoration.

In the aftermath of these photo sessions, I've found myself responding to color more deeply than before. When I see it, I can feel my eyes drinking it in. When the environment is drab, I thirst for more robust visual nourishment. This doesn't make my job any easier when I'm hired to photograph a place with lifeless color. I might have to require good color for all my future assignments, or work on more books with Susan Sargent.

—Eric Roth, December 2001

Dream
Design
Decorate

Dream Weaving

I have always enjoyed making and decorating things. When I was a small child, I was constantly drawing, doodling, and making things with fabric. I'm not really sure when my fascination with textiles started, although I can remember having a box of fabric swatches—fragments, really—by the time I was fourteen. I loved to go to junk stores where I could root through racks and trunks of old clothes, curtains, and table linens, imagining the stories that might lie behind a piece of beaded brocade or delicate embroidery.

When I was about fifteen, I took up batik, learning from an artist friend at her house after school. We spent hours up to our elbows in dyes in an old-fashioned bathtub, playing with colors and patterns. We mounted our fabrics on stretch frames for wall hangings and sewed them up into pillowcases—my first "applied arts" experience. A few years later, I turned my skills in making fabrics into a summer business, creating batik clothing for a store on Martha's Vineyard. I also did some silk-screening (the process was too fussy for me; trying to get the register right drove me crazy), and I made and sold wall hangings. By this time I was developing an interest in weaving and was desperate to learn to work on a loom. I read books and tried to understand the intricacies of harnesses and threads, but I needed a teacher.

I finished high school in the summer of Woodstock. (If you rent the movie, you can see me clapping and singing along with Country Joe and the Fish—my 1.5 seconds of fame.) That fall I enrolled in college with a dual major in English and art. Two dull years later, I seemed to be majoring in photography, which was fascinating but not what I wanted to do for a career. The college didn't offer any courses in textiles, the subject I really wanted to study, but I found a program in Scandinavia through a friend, who assured me I could learn weaving there. So I high-tailed off for a junior year abroad in northern Sweden.

Swedish Sojourn

The school that offered the weaving program was in Dalarna ("Dalacarlia" in English), a province located about 350 miles north of Stockholm. It was rural, with a local economy based first on agriculture and then on handicrafts. The area was and is famous for its charming landscapes, folk textiles, beautiful woodcarvings, and rustic crafts—and its interminable, dark winters. I fell in love with the folk culture there, with the way all of the people lived close to the land and were so connected to their cultural history. Many people still lived in traditional Swedish log houses, some of them hundreds of years old, and tended beautiful little gardens and orchards. Weaving and other kinds of handwork were regarded as just ordinary parts of daily life.

"THE ARTIST IS THE MAN WHO CREATES NOT ONLY FOR NEED BUT FOR JOY."

Roger Fry, art critic and painter, 1869–1934

I had seen only one loom up close in my life, except in museums, and when I walked into the school's weaving room, where twenty-five large floor looms were lined up, I felt I had arrived, at last, in heaven. Learning to weave (and to speak Swedish) kept my spirits up during that long dark winter, which makes New England's pale by comparison. I have no doubt that my love of color grew by leaps and bounds during those long months.

I had initially expected to return home at the end of the school year, but I was offered a summer apprenticeship at a small textile mill in the area. The mill was (and still is) owned by the Wålstedt family. On the adjoining farm, they raised Lantras sheep, a rare breed that produces a fine long-staple wool, which we spun into yarn at the mill.

Anna Wålstedt, the most extraordinary person I have ever known, taught me how to dye. As a commercial by-eye (no formula) dyer, I honed my eye for colors under the pressure of responsibility, because it was up to me to make sure the day's orders turned out right. We filled orders for many of Sweden's most prominent artists and textile companies. The custom work required us to keep adjusting the colors until we achieved a certain level of harmony within the group. My coworkers were masters of dyeing, and I could have had no better training.

The Wålstedts also did custom weaving of blankets, throws, and traditional Swedish textiles for bedcovers and woolen table runners, so I was able to improve my weaving skills. But after a year at the mill, I wanted to go back to school to learn the

ABOVE: *I cultivated my eye for color at one of my first jobs, dyeing yarn at a Swedish textile mill. These colorful skeins in my studio were dyed for various tapestry projects.*

RIGHT: *The tools of my trade: yarns, sketchbooks, and rug designs.*

skills for tapestry weaving. I enrolled in a one-year textile-degree program at a school in nearby Leksand, the first American to go there.

I studied intermediate-to-expert weaving, including drafting (how to set up the loom), textile theory, and industrial textile design. In the evening, at home in the tiny two-room cottage I was renting, I would practice on a nineteenth-century floor loom I had bought at an auction for ten dollars. I began weaving tapestries, inexpertly, realizing that I had a long way to go before I could execute the designs in my head. Still, I made progress. Some of these early tapestries were shipped to the United States to be sold through a gallery. They actually did sell, and the gallery asked for more. I was becoming increasingly entranced by the texture of a woven surface, and believed I had found my lifelong career. In my dreams I saw myself as another Hannah Ryggen or Helena Hernmarck—famous tapestry artists of Scandinavia.

I ended up staying in Sweden for four years, all filled with learning different aspects of textile design. By the end, I had also developed a pretty clear vision of the kind of life I wanted. I aimed to live simply on a small farm, weaving tapestries and raising sheep, but I couldn't find such a place in Sweden. (Farms there are handed down from generation to generation and are rarely available to a newcomer, let alone a foreigner.) Neither was there an American-style gallery system that I could use to sell my work. So I packed up my two antique looms, my yarn collection, and all my worldly goods, and left the little village of Dala-Floda for the United States.

A recent photo of me taken in front of the yarn bin in my studio.

A Farm in Vermont

Years before, my father and uncle had bought a farm in southern Vermont as a vacation home. (They had paid about fifty dollars an acre at the time.) The property included an empty rental house and five hundred or so acres of unused farmland. That's where I went to live a homesteader's life in the summer of 1975—me, my beau at the time, and a dozen Romney Marsh sheep.

I lived in that little house for four years, establishing myself as a weaver by selling tapestries through galleries in Vermont and New York, while filling gaps in my cash flow with other jobs. Serendipitous part-time work included stints as a magazine photo researcher and editor, a museum curator, and a bookstore clerk. (Skills learned through the photography job later proved enormously useful in developing marketing materials for my business.)

In 1979, my family put the farm up for sale, and after extensive politicking within the family, I arranged to buy a corner of it—forty-nine acres of woods and rolling pasture. It was—and is—stunningly beautiful, with sheltering woods to the north and east, open pasture and hay fields to the south and west, and a view across miles of Mettowee Valley farmland. There were no neighbors or even lights in sight. It took me months to adjust to the idea that I actually owned such a wonderful place. It did have one drawback, however: There were no buildings on the property.

Necessity and inclination prompted me to be frugal in designing a house. I couldn't afford to make it any larger than required to house me and my yarns, books, and looms. My years in winter-dark Sweden had taught me to appreciate simple, functional wooden houses oriented to capture as much natural light as possible. They had also accustomed me to wood stoves and outhouses. My housing needs were pretty basic.

Since I owned only a few pieces of furniture, my standards being high and my disposable income low, I designed the house around what I had. I cut out pieces of colored paper to represent my old Swedish wooden bed, my two looms, a wood stove, a wonderful (if shabby) old painted French armoire, and twelve running feet of floor-to-ceiling bins for yarn. I moved the pieces of paper around on a floor plan to see what arrangement would work best. Then I hired a local builder of post-and-beam houses to work with me, and we designed a small house to fit my needs and my budget of eleven thousand dollars, loaned by my mother.

I wound up with a straightforward design for a tiny house, eighteen feet wide, twenty feet long, and one and a half stories high. I used salvaged windows and doors, which helped determine the window placement. The house had only two rooms, one up and one down. Half of the downstairs was my workspace, with my loom and shelves for wool. The other half served as my living space: kitchen, living room, and dining room in one. Upstairs, tucked under the steep-pitched roof, was my bedroom and "library," with twenty feet of bookcases on the north wall. (I am a voracious reader.) I had no bathroom that first year, just a tidy little outhouse in a grove of maples a short walk from the house. Friends gathered to raise the post-and-beam frame in the fall of 1979, and I planned to move in by Thanksgiving, finished or not. With the outhouse, an outdoor well, and a wood stove, I could make do and continue building and beautifying the house as time passed.

By the Thanksgiving deadline, the walls were insulated, plasterboard hung, and I had frozen my fingers nailing wooden shingles onto the exterior walls. It was minimalist housing at first—a lot like camping in a wilderness cabin—but it was my dream come true. That house was to be my home and a constant work in progress for the next seventeen years.

I married a year after I moved in, and my husband and I built a small addition onto the west side of the house, including a kitchen, a tiny pantry, and a bathroom. Our son, Max Cooper, was born in 1981, and a few years later we designed another, bigger addition, again doing much of the finish work ourselves. By the time our second son, Ben, arrived in 1985, we were mostly done—with construction. We still hadn't really started the creative decorating required to make the space our own.

Susan Sargent Designs

Like the house, my professional life was also expanding. For twenty years I had concentrated on weaving large, one-of-a-kind tapestries, twelve to thirty feet square, many of which now hang in museums and private collections. One large commission was a tapestry eight feet wide and seventeen feet long, which required a new, larger Swedish loom and took me a year to complete. My work was chosen for an international tapestry show; I was part of a show at the Textile Museum in Washington, DC; and one of my works appeared in a new book on contemporary tapestry. Demand for my work began to exceed what I could accomplish with one pair of hands. I had reached a crossroads in my work life; I had to either hire and train studio assistants or branch out in some other way.

In 1992, an old friend who had a small import/export business asked me to design and produce a collection of tapestry pillows for him, based on my designs for wall hangings. I had to go to Europe to find people with the skills needed to make the pillows, and wound up giving the assignment to a women's weaving cooperative in Hungary. Developing the designs and working with other weavers to produce them turned out to be complicated and demanding, but I discovered I had exactly the right skills to get the job done. I was a hands-on artisan, designer, and colorist, and I had a distinctive style that seemed to transfer nicely to new categories of products.

I liked the travel, the exposure to different cultures, and the challenge of dealing with other production workshops. I had found what I wanted to do next. The following year I designed and licensed a line of woven and knotted rugs, this time traveling to India to work with a weaving company there. Almost before I realized it, I was as involved in design and manufacturing as I had been in my own hands-on tapestry business.

ABOVE AND OPPOSITE: *Organza and appliqué pillows, hand-painted bed linens, and woven and tufted rugs were among my first products when I launched Susan Sargent Designs in 1995. The product line eventually expanded to include all kinds of home furnishings. (Photos by John Owens.)*

Designing textile products for the home had begun as a sideline but turned into my primary business in 1995, as I took the next logical step and launched my own design, production, and marketing company, Susan Sargent Designs. I hired a few people to work with me, and we started with a small line of woven and hand-tufted rugs, appliqué pillows and coverlets, and hand-painted bed linens, all made in India. I began to travel to India regularly to check samples and oversee production. The designs reflected some of my favorite themes: nature, gardening, farm animals, circuses, and architecture, all in vivid colors.

I was now part of the home-furnishings industry as a wholesaler, with all that implied. I went to trade shows, developed a sales catalog, hired a sales manager and regional sales reps, and dove headlong into wholesaling imported textile products. Soon the collection expanded to include ceramics hand-painted in China and Italy, blown glassware from Poland, and painted furniture. After a couple of years, my products were carried in about a thousand high-end stores nationwide, mostly boutiques specializing in home furnishings. The products were also featured in major catalogs such Neiman Marcus, Macy's, Saks Fifth Avenue, Garnet Hill, Orvis, and

Colonial Williamsburg. Our annual sales had climbed to several million dollars, and I found myself working in a real office, with a staff of twelve, ringing telephones, a Rolodex, a desktop calendar, and meetings.

For someone who had spent twenty years making things alone in her studio, shifting to a design and management role was infinitely challenging, often rewarding, and sadly incomplete. I was used to being able to step back at the end of each day and see something tangible that I had accomplished: so many new design sketches, or a certain number of inches of weaving. Now design sessions were intermittent; "finished" products were months away from being real. The actual work was no longer under my eye or in my hands.

While I have always worked to make my house interesting and colorful, I date my transformation into an incorrigible house-tweaker from the moment I stopped making something with my hands each day. Now I'll paint something at home on the spur of the moment, just for the joy of using a brush. I'll dream of projects and wake up with ideas for a curtain, a bureau, or a painted floor I need to tackle. It's not unusual for me to enlist my groaning family to help rearrange the furniture, which will trigger some other change in paint or fabric. My house is indeed constantly changing; it is eternally, happily, a work in progress.

That's it: the autobiography of Susan Sargent (so far), abridged. I think now you'll be able to recognize where many of the ideas discussed and pictured in this book came from. My art reflects my life. I hope the ideas presented here will encourage others to follow their own creative paths and find great joy in the journey.

Just a few of the dozens of designs I've created for tufted and hooked rugs. Bird Tree (top row, center) and Circling Ducks (middle row, center) are two of my favorites.

The Drive to Decorate

I love the concept of decoration, but hate the word *decorating*. It has been sadly trivialized by overuse. Applied now to absolutely everything from hanging ornate curtains to making fancy cakes, it has fallen out of favor because of its commonness, to be replaced by the more important-sounding *home design*. The problem with *home design* is that it implies a master plan. The very definition of *design,* according to *Webster's New Collegiate Dictionary,* is "to conceive and plan out in the mind." That doesn't sound like my approach.

When I think of a way to beautify my home, I usually just do it without having any larger scheme in mind—not in my conscious mind, anyway. That clearly falls under the definition of *decorate*—"to furnish with something ornamental"—rather than *design.* We're talking about a simple process here: You start with an object or piece of furniture or wall or architectural detail and decorate it to make it beautiful, fun, color-ful, or at least more interesting. The level of skill brought to the task and the amount of thought preceding it are less important than the desire and confidence to do it.

The word *decoration* has a wonderful and venerable history. It entered the English language in the early sixteenth century, coming indirectly from the Latin *decorare,* which means "to add honor or ornament." Decoration might refer to anything from simple folk patterns painted on a chair to the most incredible craftwork of a Renaissance master furniture-maker. Decoration can be done on a small scale—in the detail on a carved spoon or gold brooch, for example—or on one as grand as palazzo-level ornamentation.

It seems that in every culture and every age of the world, people have felt a com-pulsion to decorate their surroundings. I have always been intrigued by the carving and painting in early Nordic wooden houses, done centuries ago with the simplest of

"A HOME IS NOT SOME LIFELESS OBJECT, BUT IS ALIVE AND LIKE ALL LIVING THINGS IT MUST OBEY THE LAW OF LIFE AND MUST CHANGE FROM MOMENT TO MOMENT."

Carl Larsson, painter, 1853–1919

ABOVE: *Anything can afford an opportunity for spontaneous decoration—even the inside of a cupboard door. Here, I painted a list of the cupboard's contents right on top of the vintage door's original paint.*

RIGHT: *A plain white room is a good showcase for brightly colored fabrics. The matching wooden beds in this guest room belonged to my grandfather.*

tools and pigments. In the course of lives that were grueling and short, people still found time to make their houses personal and beautiful. As the genome-mapping project proceeds, I suspect scientists will find the specific gene that makes us dream about how we want our homes to look and inspires us to keep moving the furniture around and painting, reupholstering, and trimming everything we own.

Our homes should never be finished; like us, they will always be works in progress. The wonderful thing about that is that we can feel absolutely free to decorate our surroundings in any way that expresses who we are today. And we should feel just as free to redecorate them to express who we are tomorrow.

Decorating is an art, not a science. We all have our own sense of what is beautiful, comfortable, and appropriate, and assembling all of the elements that will make our ideal room is largely an intuitive process. As I see it, decorating simply means taking advantage of opportunities, large and small, to make your home more beautiful. You don't need a large bank account or an art-school background, just some paint, some fabric, an idea, and your own sense of style.

If you've read many home-design and decorating books, you've undoubtedly encountered a lot of rules about what you should and shouldn't do. Forget them. I can think of only one rule or principle that I would confidently declare to be applicable in every situation: The work is never finished. It is as necessary to keep embellishing our environment as it is to keep breathing. If we ever stopped looking at, thinking about, and fiddling with the things that surround us, our lives and our homes would quickly become sterile and dull.

Hand-painted ceramics in a lively Blue Leaf pattern were part of my first Italian pottery collection (see "How to Do It: Painted Ceramics" on page 53).

THOUGHTS (NOT RULES) ON DECORATING

Here are some thoughts (not rules) to repeat like a mantra any time you find yourself hesitating to try out a decorating idea because you're afraid of making a mistake:

- Your space is a reflection of yourself. It will never be finished or perfect. Like you, it will always be a work in progress.
- You don't have to plan everything down to the last detail before you start. Try anything that appeals to you and see where it takes you.
- Small projects can have as much impact and satisfaction as a major renovation.
- Open your eyes to color. Don't let the color police sway you from mixing and matching in any way that seems right to you. If you rent a house or apartment and can't paint the walls, paint your furniture. If you can't paint the furniture, fill the place with bright cushions and curtains.
- Be flexible. It's not necessary for furniture or towels or dinnerware to match. You can combine old and new, formal and casual, simple and fanciful. Mix everything up and surprise yourself.
- Make sure that you like everything in your home enough to look at it every day. If it's not functional or beautiful, let it go.
- If you can't find what you want or can't afford it, then make it, paint it, strip it, or fake it. It's not necessary to attain the ideal in a single leap; you could just take one step closer.
- If your house or apartment doesn't make you smile when you walk in the door—if you can't feel it saying, "Welcome home!"—something is missing.

Living Color

"I FEEL THROUGH COLOR."

Henri Matisse, artist, 1869–1954

It's surprising to me how many people are utterly lacking in confidence when they have to make choices about colors. "I just don't have a good eye for color," they might say, as they dial up a decorator for help. And they might be right: Some people undoubtedly do have color vision that is more finely tuned than others', in the same way that some people have perfect pitch. But people who don't have perfect pitch can usually still pick out a new CD without consulting an expert. I think we should approach color choices the same way.

True, you might not want to spend a fortune on an expensive rug or wallpaper if you are not entirely confident about the color, but there is no reason not to take a chance on paint. I love paint because it is relatively cheap, easy to use, and easy to cover up if I blow it (nobody gets it right every time). And while I have often brought home a can of paint and then decided not to use it for the purpose I'd intended, I don't think I've ever picked a color that I couldn't eventually use somewhere.

Color, more than anything else, makes your living space special. When a room makes an immediate, positive impression on me, it's usually because of the colors that were used. Give me a vibrantly colored room full of beautiful things, impeccably arranged, and I will inevitably be drawn to the color before I notice the contents.

Given the emphasis I place on color, you might find the following a strange confession: The first time I had a whole house of my own to paint, I painted every wall white. Pregnant with my second child, I was hurrying to move in and, as I had to do all the painting myself (not a pretty sight), I hadn't the time or energy to think beyond neutral walls. In addition, I was an artist with gallery aspirations, and white seemed the best choice as an unobtrusive background for my work.

My family lived in white rooms for years before I got around to repainting. Still, my yarns and vivid tapestries provided startling color in these simple spaces, and the effect was far from tame. I still like white walls and still like to make a splash with bright fabrics, but I've also expanded my horizons because of the sheer pleasure of transforming a room with paint in surprising colors.

Overcoming Chromatophobia

Chromatophobia is a word I made up myself, although I wouldn't be surprised to learn that it actually existed. I'm defining it as a condition that afflicts many people when they approach a decorating project. The first colors they think of are vivid and exciting, but after shuffling through hundreds of paint chips, they settle on white with just a touch of some indeterminate hue and a name like Goat's Breath or Pollen Dust. They long for color, but they're afraid to use it.

When and why does chromatophobia set in? It certainly doesn't afflict children; they instinctively reach for the brightest crayons. I believe we should use color in our homes the way a child uses it in a coloring book and nature uses it outside: lavishly, boldly, and in unexpected combinations.

Colors affect all of us—not just children—on an emotional level. Even when we aren't conscious of it, the colors that surround us influence how we feel and even how well we function. Many studies have demonstrated that people respond to colors in fairly predictable ways. We are likely to find red stimulating; green, restful; blue, calming; yellow, energizing; orange, welcoming. It's interesting to be aware of those associations, but don't let them influence you too much. Your home is not a psychology lab, and the responses that matter are the ones you actually feel, not the ones some study predicts you will feel.

I often use bedrooms for my color experiments. Here, I combined mango-yellow walls, a lilac floor, and a pale blue-green baseboard. If you aren't sure about your color choices, take it one step at a time, starting with the wall and painting a patch to see if you like the color.

Making Color Choices

I doubt there is ever just one right color for a painting project. Of the thousands of colors available, you can usually find a number that would work perfectly well, so you needn't face a color decision fearing that it's a basic choice between good and evil. Even with that weight removed, making a selection among so many alternatives can be difficult, so here are a few useful techniques to help you narrow the choices:

CONSIDER THE CHARACTERISTICS OF THE ROOM. How large is it? How much natural light does it get? What direction does it face? What will it be used for? What time of day are you usually in that room, and who is likely to be with you: guests, family, the dog?

THINK ABOUT THE THINGS YOU EXPECT TO HAVE IN THE ROOM. Do they suggest a color scheme to you? If so, great; that can make your decision simpler. If not, don't worry about it. Don't be bullied by your possessions. I never let existing furniture or fabric colors prevent me from using a wall color I really like. Furniture can be painted or reupholstered or replaced, and often all it takes is the addition of a few bright pillows to tie the old colors to the new.

TEST SOME COLORS. Go to a paint store and grab one of the last best bargains: paint chip cards. You can take as many as you want. I keep bags of them in my files and group them roughly by color groups: all the blue-violets together, all the lime greens, all the yellows and oranges, all the taupes and grays. I collect paint chips the way my brothers used to collect baseball cards, and I gloat over them with exactly the same delight. When I come across a new paint line, like the British Farrow and Ball or Jane Churchill, I add them to my collection.

LEFT: *This little mantelpiece village is a reminder that unexpected color combinations can create surprisingly harmonious effects.*

OPPOSITE: *Bright cotton hangings create an intimate alcove in this one-room guest cottage. Fabrics can be used casually in a variety of ways to contribute texture and color to any decorating scheme.*

After you've gone through your paint chips and picked a few colors you'd like to try, take the sample chips to the paint store and ask the clerk to match them. Try some safe and conservative colors if you like, but be sure to try at least one killer color, too. Any paint store can match chips from any paint company, and while they won't always get it just right (pigments are generally much better in more expensive paints) you can get very close if you are dealing with a knowledgeable clerk at a good store.

Some paint suppliers, like Dulux, are even more helpful. They have little sample bottles of stock colors available for free. These hold enough paint to cover an area a couple of feet square. Otherwise, you'll have to invest in a quart of paint in any color you want to test at home.

Many of my decorating projects start with a trip to the paint cupboard to see what colors I have on hand. Choosing the right color is largely an experimental process; I might try two or three before I find one I really like.

COLOR THEORY IN A NUTSHELL

Cast your mind back to high school science class and the experiment with the prism. The prism separated the colors in sunlight by wavelength, forming a band with red (the shortest visible wavelength) at one end and violet (the longest) at the other. If you join the two ends of that band together, you have a color wheel, a tool used by decorators to show how colors relate to one another.

The three primary colors—red, yellow, and blue—can be mixed together to make every other color on the wheel. Mixing two primary colors gives you one of three secondary colors: orange, green, or purple. Mixing two of those yields one of six tertiary colors. You can go on mixing indefinitely, getting more and more subtle variations at each stage.

Using clear colors as they appear on a standard color wheel is incredibly boring if you're painting a room. During my career as a dyer in a Swedish woolen mill, I learned to take the edge off a too-bright shade by adding tiny amounts of pigment: a drop of gray or blue to soften a red, for example. When you move slightly away from clear shades, you get more intriguing interpretations of the colors.

My own palette (shown below) is quite eccentric. I have eliminated colors I don't like and would never use, like Kelly green and royal blue. All of my reds veer toward orange; all of the blues toward violet. My greens are on the yellow side, and my yellows on the warm end, with quite a lot of red.

You can develop your own personal palette by sorting through color chips and organizing the ones you like as if they were on a color wheel. Add new colors as you find them; toss out others if you discover you don't like them after all. As you refine your palette, applying no standard but your own taste, you will find that the colors all tend to work together, however unlikely some combinations might seem.

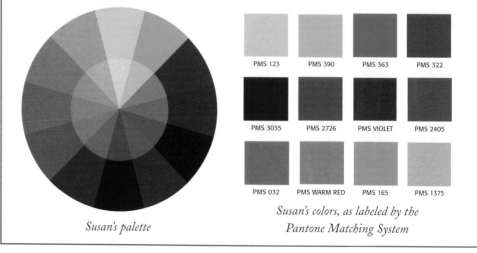

Susan's palette

Susan's colors, as labeled by the Pantone Matching System

Vivid colors bring a room to life. The combination of this exuberant tomato-red chair and the plum-colored ottoman lifts my spirits whenever I walk into my living room. Notice that the carpet is pretty subdued; not everything needs to shout.

I usually test colors by putting them right on the wall, covering a fairly large area—three or four square feet—so I can see what a large block of the color will look like. Sometimes I'll paint patches on several different walls, if the room has a sunny wall and a shadowy corner, for example. I look at each test area in the morning and at night to see how the color strikes me in different light. If I decide not to use a color, there's no great harm done; I'll just paint over it with the next color I test.

If it makes you nervous to put a color you are not sure about directly on the wall, paint a large piece of poster board instead. Pin it to the wall, and look at it over the course of a day or two. Move it around to look at it in various light conditions or next to different furnishings. Give yourself a little time with each color. This is a good way to narrow the choices and avoid surprises, because sometimes a large block of color on the wall looks very different than you thought it would when you chose the color chip.

If the first few colors you try don't work out, the tests won't be in vain. Each one will give you a better idea of what you want, and your next choice will probably be closer to the mark. I recently went through this process before painting an entry hall, and it saved me from distempering the wall orange, which had seemed like a good idea but wasn't.

Just keep a wary eye on yourself to make sure you're not instinctively toning down colors you really like. That's a sure symptom of chromatophobia. Avoid it like the plague.

Getting Started

OPPOSITE: *To decorate a bedroom at our beach cottage, I distempered the head-board walls with my favorite blue. I painted the antique wicker and wooden furniture, using either glossy white or colors suggesting the sea. The floor was also painted with several coats of high-gloss enamel.*

If you don't lie awake at night, as some of us do, thinking of things you want to do to your home, you might need some help getting started on a decorating project. Many of us find an interior designer to be a good resource when we're facing a big project, but the truth is, we'd really rather do it ourselves. And for small projects, that designer probably won't be available.

We are inundated with wonderful books about interiors and with "shelter" magazines full of pictures of impossibly perfect houses. These books and magazines are wonderful sources of ideas (taken with a grain of salt). I am an obsessive magazine reader and also a compulsive clipper, ripping out any photo that shows a color or fabric or idea that I like. I have developed a system to keep track of all this great stuff, after putting up with disorganized and useless piles, too time-consuming to sort through, for far too long.

What I now do is simple and quick. I buy three-ring binders, 8- by 11-inch card stock or paper in a slightly heavy weight, and economy-weight sheet protectors in boxes of one hundred sleeves. (All of these things are available at any office-supply store.) I glue each clipping onto a card or piece of paper with a glue stick, pop it into a plastic sleeve, and place the sleeve in the binder.

I collect similar types of information—about lamps, for example, or wallpapers—in separate sections of the binder, but the whole thing is so easy to flip through that you don't need to spend an undue amount of time organizing. When I tackle a large project, like a new kitchen, I can pull out the relevant pages and put them into a project binder, which reduces the amount of information I have to sift through to a manageable and useful level.

A project binder is a good place to collect all kinds of information relevant to the task at hand—not only clippings from magazines and newspapers, but also measurements and design sketches, paint chips and fabric swatches, notes or brochures about products you might want to use, and before and after photos. When I was redecorating an entire house (see *Pulling It All Together: Grover Farm,* pages 144–157), I collected tons of information about paints, wallpapers, flooring, shelving, and a dozen other subjects; a project binder kept all of the information easily on hand.

Another way to collect decorating ideas is to walk around your house or apartment with a notebook and itemize everything you want to change. You might make a note of projects as simple as adding some bright pillows to your living room couch or painting a door for a splash of color. By the time you finish your tour, you could have a long list of little things (and maybe some big ones) you'd like to change. You might even know exactly how you want to change some of them. In that case, pick a project and dive right in. If it doesn't involve explosives or a chain saw, you needn't be too afraid of making mistakes. Paint, in particular, is cheap and wonderfully forgiving.

Entryways, Halls, and Stairways

It usually takes a couple of minutes for me to walk from my car to the door of the farmhouse, although I could cover the distance in about fifteen seconds if I was in a hurry. I cross the unpaved country driveway from the garage, follow a curving flag-stone walk under a pair of ancient maple trees, and climb the granite steps to the porch. I'll say hello to the dogs and pause for a moment to gaze across the fields that slope away to the west. Sometimes I'll drop my stuff on one of the porch chairs and keep going, out to the stone terrace at the back, to watch cloud shadows sweeping over the distant line of hills. Or I might pause to pull a weed or two in the plantings that surround the house. In any case, by the time I walk through my door, my mind is at home, not back at the office or on the road.

The short walk to the house marks an important transition away from the demands and concerns of the world outside and into the private domain I share with my family. Like most New Englanders, we never use the real front door, but head automatically for the door that opens into the kitchen. We step inside, close the door behind us, and we are in our sanctuary—safe and at rest.

That transition is vital to me, but it is important also for visitors. The walk across the driveway and the lawn gives them a chance to take in the setting, to see where they are going and anticipate their reception at the door. In the meantime, they are making the mental adjustment from traveling to arriving.

"HOME IS AN INVENTION ON WHICH NO ONE HAS YET IMPROVED."
Ann Douglas, writer, b. 1942

LEFT: *Even the entrance to a stone barn is inviting when it welcomes visitors with a well-tended walkway and a comfortable garden seat.*

OPPOSITE: *The front door to our former office building is flanked by a pair of painted planters. I found the wooden tubs at a local garden center, painted them blue, and over-laid the base color with a simple pattern to give them some personality. I used the same colors in a freehand wave pattern on the risers of the stairs in the entry hall.*

Visitors form their first impression of a home during that walk to the door. To make sure it is a positive one, the approach should be both pleasant and obvious, leaving no doubt about the route one is expected to take. A gateway, a sidewalk, or just a path bordered by flowers or shrubs will signal people that they are going the right way and help them to feel at ease. Even if the door is only a few steps from the street or driveway, or is off an apartment hallway, a small porch, an outside seat, or a few plants in large tubs will reinforce the visitor's realization that this is the threshold of your home, a significant border that is about to be crossed.

The area just inside the door is a second important transition point, especially here in the Northeast, where coming indoors or going out can be quite a production in the winter. The entry hall—or these days, most likely, a mudroom—sets a mood that will influence how people feel about being in your home. It also gives visitors their first glimpse into the interior of your domain.

ABOVE: *In many country houses, the most often used entrance is a back door opening into a utility area or mudroom. Here, a window seat provides a convenient perch for pulling boots on or off.*

HOW TO DO IT Decorated Walls

One way to lighten the impact of a large block of strong color is to break it up with a painted design. That's what my friend Christine Miles did in this entry hall inside the back door of her Vermont home. Christine's airy pattern of drifting black oak leaves and bright yellow speckles keeps the crimson walls from overwhelming the small room.

Christine painted her leaf designs free-hand, which contributes to the informal effect, but you can also buy or make stencils to create similar decorative figures. You'll need either acrylic paints or Japan paints, both commonly used for stenciling, and stencil brushes or artist's brushes.

It's best to settle your color choices and have an idea of the overall pattern before you begin. For example, Christine had to choose not only her colors, but also how large the leaves would be, how many she wanted in a given area, and how far apart they would be. If you're having trouble making such decisions, try painting some sample figures from your pattern on paper and then taping them to the wall to see how they look.

Once you start laying down the design, focus on one color at a time. For Christine's pattern, this meant painting all of the black

leaves first, then going back to add their center veins and the golden speckles.

Don't panic if you make a mistake. You might be able to erase the smudge or smear with a damp cloth (for water-based paint), or just paint over the mistake with a couple of coats of the background color and then try again once the paint is dry.

OPPOSITE: *I promised Ed the dog he could be in my book. He's enjoying his supper in a colorful mudroom at the home of his owners, Christine and Joe Miles.*

The stone walk at my house leads to a side porch and this kitchen door. The massive pine sideboard is a convenient place to deposit bags of groceries or other burdens. Pegs for coats are hidden behind the door.

LEFT: *Visitors are greeted by details old and new at the Grover farmhouse. The rug is my own Hot Blocks design, and the antique settee is covered with a contemporary woven fabric. An old mirror reflects the soft blue-green distemper paint on the walls.*

OPPOSITE: *I like to use old architectural elements for decorating, particularly in entries and hallways. Clockwise from top left: the back entry to my studio; a salvaged porch railing that I used at the top of a stairway; one of several mismatched old doors in an upstairs hallway; ornate corbels that support a shelf over a back door.*

In many country houses, the principal entrance has changed over the years, often because a driveway now brings people to a side or rear door instead of to the front. Country people of the past preferred to have their houses connected to the road as directly as possible, so as to welcome in passersby for their company and conversation. Today, passing traffic feels like an intrusion, and we prefer to look away from the road and into our backyards. Consequently, many a lovely old entry hall has fallen into disuse, and guests routinely enter a country house through a messy mudroom, where the residents' lives are inartistically displayed in jumbles of boots, sports gear, and coats, with an underlayer of garden baskets and dog beds.

ABOVE: *A wide hall or stair landing is a room as well as a passageway. A big comfortable chair and my round Circus rug turn a landing in this Boston home into a cozy place for a bedtime story.*

OPPOSITE: *Patty Yoder created a perfect place for reading and conversation in her upstairs hallway. She painted all the woodwork glossy white, covered an old armchair with an antique quilt, and put a folk-art hooked rug on the floor. A pitcher full of peonies adds a dramatic burst of color.*

Our front door fell into disuse long before we acquired the house, and there is no longer even a path to it. I suspect there was once an entry hall, but now the door opens directly into our family room/library—not the room where we want to welcome guests. So when we enlarged and remodeled the kitchen, we provided for an entry area there. It's not an entry hall, but it serves the same purpose in a more casual way. Just inside the door is an old sideboard where people can set down groceries or anything else they might be carrying; under the sideboard are several large plastic bins for shoes and boots. On the wall immediately to the right of the door are two rows of hooks for jackets, pocketbooks, briefcases, or backpacks. This is certainly a more casual space than a traditional entry hall, but it is roomy and convenient, and it welcomes visitors directly into our principle social space.

When we acquired the Grover farm, the place that now houses Susan Sargent Designs and serves as a family guest house, we found a wonderful entry hall that was intact but unused. The elegant front door, flanked by sidelights with ancient panes of rippled glass, was practically hidden behind overgrown cedars. It clearly had not been the main entry for decades. We took down the dark trees, uncovering not only the door but also a pretty pair of marble steps, and refurbished the interior to make the hall friendly and bright. Although this no longer a functioning entry, it is once again a bright and pleasant passageway between the two levels of the house. (For more about the Grover farm, see pages 144–157.)

A true entry hall is both a passageway and a room, and it deserves as much attention to decoration as you would give to any other public room. If there is space available, the hall can be furnished with a few pictures or bits of furniture that will give it your personal stamp, making family members feel immediately at home and helping visitors form an impression of the house and its occupants.

More practical details have to be considered, too. There should be a shelf or table so people can put things down while they take off their coats (or put them on) and a closet or shelves and hooks to collect outdoor gear. It's also nice to have a bench or chair where people can sit to deal with their boots or wait for someone else who is getting ready to go out. In fact, I like to put seats and small tables or bookcases in any passageway that is wide enough for them. A seat makes a hallway or stair landing a place in its own right, not just a space to move through on your way to somewhere else.

Staircases, whether in an entry hall or another passageway, also afford special opportunities for decoration. An open staircase adds height and a little drama to a hall—an effect that can be enhanced by painting the risers with eye-catching accents. A stairway often affords the largest stretch of uninterrupted wall space in the home, which can be painted in a clear color of its own or decorated with stencils or freehand designs. It is also ideal for an arrangement of family photos, children's artwork, or wall hangings that might not fit on an ordinary wall.

Carl Larsson and Lilla Hyttnäs

The cottage I rented when I was working in Sweden was only twenty miles or so from the village of Sundborn in the rustic province of Dalarna. Occasionally I would drive over there in my ancient three-cylinder Saab to visit the rambling house that has justifiably been called "the national home of Sweden." This house belonged to Sweden's best-known artist, Carl Larsson, from 1888 until his death in 1919. It was the backdrop for the dozens of watercolor paintings he published in two extremely popular books: *Ett Hem* (*At Home*) and *At Solsidän* (*A House in the Sun*).

Larsson might be described as Sweden's less saccharine version of Norman Rockwell. He produced hundreds of drawings and watercolor paintings depicting the pleasures of family, home, and community. Those collected in *Ett Hem* and *At Solsidän* chronicle the everyday activities of his own large family in and around the Sundborn cottage, which was known as Lilla Hyttnäs.

Larsson and his wife, Karin, a weaver and painter, were part of Sweden's National Romantic Movement, which was similar to the Arts and Crafts Movement in England. The National Romanticists celebrated the values of a traditional, rural way of life that was disappearing with industrialization, as countless Swedes abandoned their villages and farms and moved to larger towns or emigrated to the United States.

Lilla Hyttnäs, now maintained as a national landmark, is itself a significant work of art. The rooms glow with clear, strong colors: deep blues and reds and greens. Walls, woodwork, and doors are exuberantly painted in a sophisticated folk style based on what Larsson called "all those cheery peasant patterns." He personalized every room with painted friezes, portraits of family members, and flowing inscriptions embellished with flowers. (As he suffered from depression for most of his life, I've often wondered if those painting projects helped to cheer him up.)

Larsson won significant recognition as a painter and illustrator in his lifetime, but he was never rich. He and Karin furnished their home simply, with a mismatched collection of old tables, chairs, and cupboards, such as any of their neighbors might have owned. But the furniture is beautifully decorated with painted designs; the doors are painted with portraits, flowers, and birds; and fabrics used throughout the house were all woven by Karin.

One of the motivations for publishing *Ett Hem*, Larsson wrote, was to show what could be done in decorating "a house that was not worth much in dollars and cents and whose furnishings were worth even less." He was doing it not just to show off, he explained, but because he thought Lilla Hyttnäs might serve as a useful example for people who wanted to decorate their homes nicely but inexpensively.

In Lilla Hyttnäs, the Larssons captured the beauty and simplicity of traditional Scandinavian interior design, but took the style to a new level of artistry. I am still inspired by the bright, cozy rooms in Larsson's paintings and by the memory of my visits to his home. He taught me that a house is, or can be, an autobiographical work, not only witnessing but also recording the events that occur within its walls.

RIGHT: *The dining room in Lilla Hyttnäs features red and green paneling, put up in 1890. The portrait of Esbjörn Larsson, Carl's son, was painted on the door in 1906. (Photo © Carl Larsson gården, Sundborn.)*

OPPOSITE: *Karin's workshop in Lilla Hyttnäs. (Photo © Carl Larsson gården, Sundborn.)*

Kitchens

You probably spend more of your waking hours in the kitchen than in any other room of your home, even if you aren't fond of cooking. For most of us, the kitchen is effectively the family room, a place where people naturally settle to sip a cup of coffee, read the newspaper, sort the mail, or fidget over school assignments. More meals are eaten in kitchens than in dining rooms, and more neighborly visits take place in kitchens than in living rooms.

The isolated kitchen, hidden at the back of the house and dedicated solely to food preparation, is a relic of the days when numerous middle-class families had servants and the kitchen was the province of the hired cook. Even after the servants were gone from the houses of all but the very wealthy, many people preferred to keep the kitchen, dining room, and living room separate and distinct. Preparing meals was still viewed as a servant's task, even though it was the housewife who was now doing it, and eating in a dining room was considered more genteel than eating in the kitchen.

We can thank Frank Lloyd Wright for recognizing that the isolated kitchen was both inconvenient and inappropriate in most contemporary American homes. In the 1930s, his Usonian houses, designed for ordinary families rather than the rich, had kitchens that were half open to the family room, so the person who was cooking was no longer excluded from other activities. Wright's idea was copied and adapted by other architects and builders as the Usonian house engendered the ubiquitous ranch house. By the 1960s, open floor plans were becoming popular in homes of all architectural styles.

Today the kitchen is often the most open part of the house, enabling modern families to prepare meals, eat, entertain visitors, and engage in many other activities in one large room, just as people all over the world have done for most of human history. The kitchen has been happily restored to its rightful role as the common area at the heart of the home.

"SOME ROOMS INVITE PEOPLE TO EAT LEISURELY AND COMFORTABLY AND FEEL TOGETHER, WHILE OTHERS FORCE PEOPLE TO EAT AS QUICKLY AS POSSIBLE SO THEY CAN GO SOMEWHERE ELSE TO RELAX."

Christopher Alexander, architect, b. 1936

LEFT: *Color inspiration is where you find it. Much of the painted decoration I've done in kitchens and dining rooms has been inspired by the strong colors of fruits and vegetables.*

OPPOSITE: *In the kitchen of my first farmhouse, I painted the ceiling beams and trim a shade of blue that I'd seen in a Shaker building. The cabinets and countertop were recycled; they date from the 1950s. The tiles over the sink were purchased by my mother in Mexico before I was born.*

A Farmhouse Kitchen

Arranging a kitchen as the multipurpose room it has become is almost always a balancing act. You need an efficient, well-equipped work place for preparing meals, but you also want it to feel welcoming and comfortable, a place where people can visit or family members can work on their own projects without worrying that they are in the way. In essence, you want to re-create the feel of an old farmhouse kitchen.

That wasn't hard to do in my case, since I actually live in an old farmhouse. The original kitchen was a good-sized room, but an incredibly dreary one. It had been remodeled in the 1960s, and the walls and cupboards had been paneled with fake barn board. The floor was painted dark brown, and the ceiling was covered with unpainted plywood nailed up between exposed beams. The four windows all looked out on a wraparound porch, so sunlight never reached the room.

I couldn't bear to be in a room that dark, so remodeling the kitchen became my top priority. First the barn board and plywood came down, to be replaced by plasterboard on the walls and ceilings and simple paneled doors on the original frames of the cabinets. The dark, closed-in porch on the west side of the house was insulated and windows were added, while the interior wall was removed, adding ten feet to the kitchen's width. One corner of the expanded space was enclosed to create a large pantry, and a raised hearth was constructed in the opposite corner. On the south side of the house, the porch was rebuilt as it had been in 1840 and left open. Now instead of three windows looking onto shadowy porches, the kitchen had seven windows flooding it with light.

OPPOSITE: *This post-and-beam kitchen has a slate floor, but what really catches your eye is the violet-blue paint on the simple bead-board cabinets, a color inspired by flowers in my garden. Hand-painted tiles depicting farm animals line the wall above the sink.*

HOW TO DO IT Painted Ceramics

Some years ago I sketched some designs for a line of kitchenware: plates, bowls, pitchers, mugs, and so on. I didn't have any experience with pottery, and I wasn't sure how my designs and colors would look on ceramics, so I went to a local do-it-yourself ceramics studio to experiment a bit.

Ceramics workshops seem to have sprung up everywhere in recent years, attesting to the popularity of the craft. These shops provide a selection of unglazed pottery pieces and all of the glazes, tools, and coaching you need to create your own designs. When you have finished, you leave your pieces to be fired in the shop's kiln and return to pick them up later.

ABOVE: *Some of my own painted ceramics.*
LEFT: *Vermont potter Jane Davies.*

I painted the room in light, quiet colors: white for the ceiling, cabinets, and trim; white, too, for the walls, except around the cabinets, where I used a pale dove gray. The floor was first a strong yellow, but gray-green proved a more practical choice, considering the amount of mud the dogs bring in. The Formica countertops are a darker gray-blue.

Most kitchens contain so many interesting and beautiful objects—china, pottery, canisters, tins, glassware, and so on—that they practically decorate themselves. I use open shelves, dish rails, and cupboard tops to store and display my favorite pieces. Cooking utensils, antique or new, hanging from pegs or hooks are also interesting. Even small appliances like toasters and blenders often come in appealing shapes and colors, so they look decorative just sitting on the countertop.

I have never liked the American extreme "fitted kitchen," in which everything is a perfect match. Where is the personality in long rows of closed doors? The furniture in my kitchen includes an enormous old pine sideboard, acquired from

I love the "stuff" that goes in kitchens: glassware, pottery, canisters, and gleaming cook-ware and appliances. Glass-fronted cupboards and open shelves provide a place to store your favorite objects and display them at the same time.

an antique shop; a pair of handmade plank-bottom chairs that I brought home from Sweden; and a modern table made by a local furniture maker, which I painted in bright shades of green and yellow. Four chairs usually surround the table, but it will easily accommodate eight. This is where we eat almost all of our meals, and it is the customary assembly point for impromptu family meetings. The table also serves as an all-purpose workstation. It has been used for everything from income-tax preparation and rug design to chain saw repair, as well as ordinary kitchen tasks.

Cupboards always give me an irresistible urge to decorate. These patterns were inspired by decorations I'd seen in Charleston, the Sussex home of English artists Vanessa Bell and Duncan Grant. (For more about Charleston, see pages 128–129.)

ABOVE: *A raised Scandinavian-style hearth occupies one corner of my kitchen. It is faced with rustic Moravian tiles that a company in Pennsylvania still makes from the original molds.*

OPPOSITE: *This open Vermont kitchen draws much of its character from the mix of old and new wood, both painted and plain, used in its construction and decoration.*

Since both guests and family members seem to gravitate toward our kitchen rather than the living room, we've provided a sitting area in the fireplace corner. It's furnished with a comfortable armchair upholstered in bold hand-painted fabric, a two-seat couch piled high with colorful pillows, and a side table with a reading lamp. All in all, there is more than enough room in the kitchen for a half-dozen or more people to cook, converse, read, or snooze by the fire, all at the same time.

It's not possible to create a real farmhouse kitchen in every house or apartment. But you can strive to create that same feeling wherever you live. At the very least, you can arrange and decorate the kitchen area so it's a cheerful place to be. If it's a dull or ugly color, paint it. If it's dark, put in better lighting. Buy utensils and kitchenware that you really like and put some of your favorite things out where you can see them. Get rid of any kitchen stuff you don't like or use. Make the kitchen you have, whatever its assets or limitations, *your* kitchen—a room where you always feel at home.

HOW TO DO IT Button Wreath

This button wreath—a present from my colleagues at work—hangs in the dining area of my farmhouse kitchen. My design company had produced a line of duvet covers and pillows with button backs, and there were hundreds of fabric-covered replacement buttons left over. The wreath was a creative answer to the question, "Now what can we do with these?" Of course, everyone also contributed from their own button boxes.

To make a similar wreath, gather the following items: a wreath form made of Styrofoam or straw (available at any crafts store), a piece of black felt that's a little more than twice as large as the wreath, needle and thread, a whole bunch of buttons, and a glue gun.

You'll need to cut two pieces of felt to cover the wreath form. Fold the felt in half and place the wreath form on top. Trace lines around the inside and the outside of the form, then allow for an extra inch of material outside the outer circle, and inside the inner circle. Cut two felt "donuts" to make the front and back pieces of the cover.

Sew buttons onto the front piece until it is completely covered, leaving small uncovered borders around both edges.

Using a hot glue gun, glue the back cover onto the wreath form. Then glue the front cover onto the form, overlapping the back on both the outer and inner edges. If any part of the seam is visible when the wreath is hung on the wall, glue on a few more buttons to hide it.

Use the glue gun to attach a colorful bow as a final touch.

The Glorious Pantry

In Louis XIV's seventeenth-century palace at Versailles, where supper generally included twenty-eight dishes served in four courses, twelve rooms were reserved for the preparation of royal meals. A principal manor house at that time might have had as many as five or six rooms in a kitchen suite, including the main kitchen, a larder, a pantry, a dairy, a pastry, and a scullery. Meals are simpler today, and so are our kitchen requirements. We don't need a kitchen suite anymore, but it sure is glorious to have a pantry!

A closet just large enough to step into is certainly useful for kitchen storage, but doesn't qualify as a pantry. A real pantry requires a minimum of about sixty square feet: a space eight feet square or six by ten feet, for example. It might have open shelves from floor to ceiling on all sides, or a combination of open shelves, drawers, and a work counter. I like to have some counter space in the pantry where I can keep appliances that I don't want on display in the kitchen, such as the microwave oven and the food processor. And because I'll be using that equipment and occasionally doing other kitchen tasks right in the pantry, I like having a window and good lights.

A pantry can be a purely practical storage place, with no special decoration at all. But I have also seen some pantries that were beautifully painted and stenciled, with shelves loaded with gorgeous ceramics and gleaming pots and pans. Mine doesn't usually look like that, chaos being more the rule.

In my first pantry, I wallpapered the walls before the shelves went in and painted big red and gray diamonds on the floor. The pantry I have now isn't decorated as elaborately. The shelves are a pale grass-green, and the floor is the strong yellow that I had initially tried to use in the kitchen, but the only ornamentation is provided by the room's contents: a shelf of cookbooks; a row of old kerosene lamps; lots of glassware and dishes; colorful pottery bowls and pitchers; and canisters, jars, and cans of kitchen staples. A collection of whisks is displayed on one wall, and the light through the little window filters through colored-glass flower vases.

If you're lucky enough to have one, a pantry can become a very special little room—a perfect place to try out decorative ideas and color combinations that surprise you every time you open the door. In fact, you might just want to keep the door open all the time.

ABOVE: *The checkerboard pattern on this pantry floor has seen more than twenty years of wear, but it's still as decorative as it was when the paint was fresh. I used Old Village oil-based paint, which ages better than anything else I've tried. (See "How to Do It: Painted Floors" on page 125.)*

OPPOSITE: *A well-organized pantry is beautiful as well as practical. Everything you don't want to look at can be tucked away, and everything you do want to look at can be given pride of place on open shelves. Be sure to select a wall color that sets off your favorite things.*

My kitchen pantry is decorated only by its contents. The window is framed by my collection of old whisks, and the marble countertop beneath provides extra workspace for chopping, mixing, and other kitchen chores.

Nature

I was at a trade show, arranging some sample products in my company's booth, when I observed a woman examining one of my appliqué pillows with a thoughtful expression. Seeing that I had noticed, she smiled and said, "That's a very unusual color, but I'm sure I've seen it somewhere before; I'm just trying to remember where."

No doubt she had seen it. It's a color I see for a few days every spring, when the maples marching up the hillside beyond our pasture are just beginning to unfurl their leaves. In fact, it's one of my favorite shades of green, and it seems a shame that it lasts such a brief time each year. I have one of those pillows on a sofa in my own living room, so now I can enjoy the color any time.

People often ask me how I happened to think of using a particular color or combination of colors in one of my designs. Inspiration comes in many ways, but for me, the natural world is probably the most important source, particularly the flower borders around my house and the fields and woods where I walk every day with my dogs.

A few years ago, my house was featured in *Country Living* magazine, and I received a flood of letters asking, "Where did you find the yellow you used in the bedroom pictured on page 117?" My response was, "It's Benjamin Moore paint number 153," which is what I think they wanted to know, but isn't really the answer to their question. In fact, I found the color in a ranunculus blossom; the Benjamin Moore paint was the closest I could come to matching it.

We all have a tendency to simplify our lives by compartmentalizing things in our minds. When we want to choose colors for a room or a piece of furniture, we naturally think of colors we have seen used for those purposes elsewhere. It doesn't usually occur to us to think that the lilacs hanging outside the door might be the perfect color for a wooden chair, or the yellows, oranges, and reds in a bouquet of flowers might be the ideal combination to decorate a table.

Nature is not at all conservative in either her choice of hues or the way she combines them, but I can't recall ever looking at one of her grand displays, such as a hardwood forest in full autumn foliage, and turning away thinking, "Those colors just don't *go* together." That doesn't mean that every color you see outside belongs in your living room, but any of them can be considered.

The world outside my window is also the primary source of ideas for the images and patterns I use in decoration. Flowers, insects, animals, fish, and trees have inspired so many of my designs I can't begin to guess at the number. I'll bet I've done hundreds based on birds alone. Even many of my more abstract designs reflect shapes I found in nature: leaves, shells, beach pebbles, ripples in water.

I'm totally visually oriented. I'd like to think that everything I see—every shape, every color, every pattern—gets filed in my mind for future use. In fact, I'm sure I miss a lot. But I have tried to train myself to really pay attention when I see something that surprises me with delight, so it doesn't just flicker through my mind and disappear. I may never use it in my work, but I'll always enjoy remembering it.

"WE MAY TAKE OUR FIRST LESSONS IN COLOR FROM NATURE, ON WHOSE STOREHOUSE WE CAN DRAW LIMITLESSLY. NATURE, WHEN SHE PLANS A WONDERFUL SPLASH OF COLOR, PREPARES A PROPER BACKGROUND FOR IT . . . . A BIT OF GRAY-GREEN MOSS UPON A BLACK ROCK, A FIELD OF YELLOW DANDELIONS, A PINK AND WHITE SPIKE OF HOLLYHOCKS, AN ORANGE BUTTERFLY POISED ON A STALK OF LARKSPUR—WHAT COLOR PLANS ARE THESE!"

Elsie de Wolfe, interior decorator, 1865–1950

OPPOSITE: *The seemingly daring color scheme in this kitchen works beautifully, inspired by the brilliant oranges and purple-blues of flowers from my garden.*

Dining Rooms

One of the many choices facing anyone buying or building a home today is whether or not to have a formal dining room. *Formal*, as used by realtors and architects, really means "separate," and the case could be made that the separate dining room is a relic of the past. Certainly many new homes are being built without them, and dividing walls between kitchens and dining rooms are frequently removed in older homes during kitchen renovations. Still, according to the National Association of Homebuilders, most home buyers consider a separate dining room to be essential.

My personal feeling is that four walls do not a formal dining room make. I have seen houses in which separate dining rooms are far from formal, and others in which a very formal-feeling dining area shares space with the kitchen or living room. The key is not whether the room is separate, but the feeling you want to create in it and how you choose to decorate the space.

In the farmhouse where I live now, the kitchen is also our dining room (see overleaf). I designed the table with my friend Dan Mosheim, a master furniture maker. I had him add elements along the apron that could be painted and decorated, and I painted the top as well, using primarily yellow, black, and gray-green, with touches of other colors. The table is always a bright, cheery presence in the kitchen and a perfect setting not only for family meals, but also casual farmhouse dinners with friends.

For more formal occasions, I cover the table with an antique linen tablecloth or hand-woven place mats in rich, dark colors. With a suspended light casting a warm pool of illumination around the table, candlelight glinting off glassware and china, and the rest of the room lit only by a fire on the hearth, the setting is as elegant as anyone could desire.

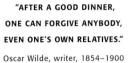

"AFTER A GOOD DINNER, ONE CAN FORGIVE ANYBODY, EVEN ONE'S OWN RELATIVES."
Oscar Wilde, writer, 1854–1900

LEFT: *This homemade drop-leaf table has been green, red, black, and is now my favorite blue. Set off by antique Vermont-made chairs, it is laid with yellow-orange fabric. The rug, dinnerware, and tall vase of flowers add even more cheery color.*

OPPOSITE: *The white wood-work and ceiling in this dining room combine with the natural wood floor to create a light and airy atmosphere. The yellow and lime green seat covers and a vase of garden flowers con-tribute colorful highlights.*

A dining room doesn't need to be separate to be formal. My dining area shares space with the kitchen, yet with the addition of dinnerware, candles, and a roaring fire, it becomes an elegant place to entertain guests. The table was made by a friend and decorated by me. The raised hearth resembles those I saw in houses throughout rural Sweden.

If a dining area doesn't have to be separate to be formal, neither is formality a requirement in a dining room that is separate. In the Grover farmhouse, for example, a formal dining room would be at odds with the rest of the house. While the dining room there is its own room, it is also a high-traffic area situated at the very center of the house (see illustrations on pages 150–151). I wanted the dining room to be simple, bright, and open, with colors and decorative accents that would tie together those used in the other rooms.

LEFT: *While this dining room is a separate room, it is hardly formal. A glass-fronted corner cupboard is an ideal showcase for favorite pieces of brightly painted ceramics.*

OPPOSITE: *An antique settee in its original green velvet and piled with bright silk cushions stands against the chalky blue and white walls of this dining room.*

RIGHT AND OPPOSITE:
Tablecloths, placemats, and
cloth napkins afford an endless
array of colors, patterns,
and textures for dining room
decoration. I enjoy bright mix–
and–match sherbet colors like
those in the linen napkins and
silk seats shown here.

HOW TO DO IT Reupholstered Chairs

Any chair with a removable seat can be reupholstered in a matter of minutes, as long as the original foam or stuffing is in good shape. Making the seat covers for this set of dining room chairs was a spur-of-the-moment project inspired by some colorful silk fabric I had left over from another job.

Remove the seat from the chair and use it as a template to mark out the pattern for the fabric. Allow an extra two inches all around so you will have enough fabric for folding and tacking under the seat.

If the seat doesn't fit too tightly in the chair's frame, you may be able to put the new cover right over the old upholstery, as I did with these chairs. But if that will make the seat too bulky to drop back into place, you will have to strip off the old upholstery and remove the tacks.

Center the seat upside down on the fabric. Starting with two opposite sides, fold the fabric over the bottom of the seat and staple it in place, using several staples on each side and folding the fabric under itself to make a half-inch hem as you go. Stretch the fabric just tight enough to compress the stuffing slightly, and alternate from side to side with the stapling. After the two sides are done, fold the corners over, fiddling with them until they are neat and square, and then staple them in place. Then do the other two sides.

Whether your taste tends toward fun or formal, adaptability is the key to creating a pleasant dining area. A sturdy table that's big enough but not overwhelming, comfortable chairs, and congenial surroundings are all you need for your family and guests to feel comfortable and at ease. Starting with those essential elements, it's easy to change the feel of the room from day to night and season to season, simply by changing the table decorations, the furniture arrangement, and the lighting. An informal space can be transformed in minutes with silk curtains, a tablecloth set with gleaming china and silver, and soft lighting from a few candles and lamps.

CLOCKWISE, FROM TOP: *A high shelf displays ceramics against a colored wall; a traditional dining room is brightened by colorful pottery on the open shelves of an old hutch; a painted armoire became a dining room cupboard in our summer cottage (for tips on painting furniture, see page 151); a collection of teapots on a country dresser.*

OPPOSITE: *The high ceiling in this dining room allows for a colorful display shelf that extends around the entire room.*

William Morris

ABOVE: *A panel in the William Morris dining room of the Victoria and Albert Museum, which is shown opposite. (Courtesy of the Trustees of the V&A. Photo by Paul Robins.)*

OPPOSITE: *A view of the stunning Morris dining room at the Victoria and Albert Museum. (Courtesy of the Trustees of the V&A.)*

I first encountered William Morris at the Victoria and Albert Museum in London when I was about twelve years old. The museum had an entire room devoted to Morris's work, and the first time I saw it, I felt as if I had wandered into some magical place. It wasn't just the colors or the designs that I found so appealing, but the way *everything* in the room was decorated on every possible surface: pianos, rugs, chairs, walls, curtains, pottery, stained-glass windows. It was unlike any craft or art I had seen. Unlike the conventional and soothing interiors I had grown up with in New England, it was stunningly original—decoration with a point of view all its own.

Morris began his career as an architect in 1856, but quickly shifted his attention to decorative design. The reason, he later explained, was his dismay at the degraded state of the decorative arts in England. "Accordingly with the conceited courage of a young man I set myself to reforming all that, and started a sort of firm for producing decorative articles," he wrote.[1]

Morris's "sort of firm," founded in 1861, became Morris & Co., and continued in business until 1940, producing at one time or another embroidered and woven tapestries, stained glass, painted ceramics, furniture, knotted and woven carpets, wallpaper, and printed textiles for curtains and upholstery. Many of the designs created by Morris and the firm's other artists are still in production today, and they have come to represent all that is most effective in the Victorian style.

For me, Morris's appeal lies as much in his philosophy as in his art. He believed that art and beauty were essential in every walk of life, as necessary as food and shelter to factory workers and the privileged class alike. He was appalled by working conditions in England's "dark Satanic mills" and envisioned a society in which men and women could take pleasure in their work, producing items that were well made, useful, and beautiful, "a happiness to the maker and the user."[2] Morris tried very hard to make his own company conform to that vision.

Famous for his energy and capacity for work, Morris was more likely to be found at a workbench or loom than at a desk. He particularly loved weaving and regarded tapestry as "the noblest of the weaving arts."[3] The use of tapestry hangings for home decoration had been out of fashion for more than a hundred years when Morris began working on designs to be produced by his company. Many of these designs depict classical and idealized subjects, but it is the borders and backgrounds that appeal most to me. These are alive with the flowers, vines, fruit trees, birds, and animals that are also found in his designs for carpets and textiles.

As a tapestry weaver myself, I revere William Morris as a kind of patron saint. By validating the dignity of making beautiful and distinctive things with age-old techniques in a mass-production age, he bridged the gap between what was considered "craft" and what had been elevated to "art," an important distinction for me as I set out on my personal journey as an artist.

Interior designers can make a similar claim on Morris. His mission in life, he said, was "to revive a sense of beauty in home life" and "to restore the dignity of art to household decoration."[4] While we might argue that he went too far in decorating every available surface with busy pattern (stifling by today's standards), he brought into the public mind the idea that decorative arts, made by hand, should be a part of every home. An ambitious undertaking, but he succeeded beyond his own expectations, as Morris & Co. set new standards for taste and style in home furnishings.

[1] *Victorian Interior Design,* by Joanna Banham et al. London: Cassell, 1991, pp. 82–83.
[2] Ibid., p. 81.
[3] *William Morris Textiles,* by Linda Parry. London: Weidenfeld & Nicolson, 1983, p. 100.
[4] *Victorian Interior Design,* p. 82.

Living Rooms

I loved reading Jane Austen when I was a little girl. Her heroines and young gentle-men (even the cads) conversed in wonderfully articulate sentences that unfolded, phrase after phrase, like rose blossoms. I suspected that their ability to do this was somehow related to the elegant rooms in which the conversations took place: drawing rooms, sitting rooms, parlors, and halls in English manors and cottages. My friends and I didn't speak that way, but then we were usually hanging out in a family room that had once been a garage—hardly the sort of setting Elizabeth Bennett and Fitzwilliam Darcy would choose for their verbal sparring!

I never thought about it back then, but now it strikes me as a little odd to use so many different words to describe rooms that serve the same function. In fact, the origins of these terms are quite interesting. The oldest form of living room in England and the United States is the *hall*, a word descended from the Old Teutonic *halla*, also the origin of closely related words in every northern European language. Halla referred to anything that covered or concealed, from an acorn hull to the hull of a boat to a hall covered by a roof. The Old English form, *heall*, dates back more than a thousand years—so far back that it predates the written English language.

Originally, a hall was any large place covered by a roof. Throughout northern Europe, people who didn't live in huts lived in halls, and both were one-room affairs. But by A.D. 1200, *hall* had acquired a more specific meaning: It referred to the large public room in a palace or mansion, which would have been the first room inside the entrance. By 1600 the entrance room in any house was called a hall, even if it was not a principal room. (By then, many houses had a lobby or vestibule inside the front door.) Later, the word came to be used for any vestibule or passageway, regardless of its location in the house.

The term *parlor* came into use during the early part of the Middle Ages, derived from Old French and related to *parler*, "to speak." The first parlors were found in monasteries and convents for religious orders that required vows of silence. The parlor was a room or apartment where members of the cloistered community could converse with people from outside, or where novices could talk to one another during recreation periods.

Later, *parlor* came to refer to a room in a mansion apart from the great hall, where people could have private conversations. It was then extended to rooms in ordinary

LEFT: *I bought this old chaise longue at a tag sale for twenty-five dollars. Covered with a woven paisley fabric and strewn with pillows, it looks like it belongs in an old-fashioned sitting room.*

OPPOSITE: *This couch was abandoned in a barn that came with an old house I bought. After having the couch restored and reupholstered in purple silk, I put it in my office. I painted the walls a soft gray-green and left the door and floor just as I'd found them.*

ABOVE: *Bright silk neckroll pillows can be scattered on couches and chairs for added color and for the comfort of guests.*

OPPOSITE: *Shades of lavender, raisin, and pale green tie these funky, mismatched pieces together. The lamp shade was made by stretching orange silk over a wire form, and the sheer curtains were decorated with artist inks (see "How to Do It: Painted Sheer Curtains" at right).*

houses. In a relatively grand house, the parlor would have been a living room in the sense that we use that term today. But in a two-room cottage or small farmhouse, the parlor was simply the inner or more private room—the "best" room—and it may actually have been used as a dining room or bedroom.

The *drawing room* never had anything to do with drawing. The term is actually a shortened form of *withdrawing* room. It came into use in the sixteenth century and referred to a private room adjacent to a more public one. Primarily, it was the room into which ladies would withdraw after dinner, while the men lingered in the dining room.

Salon is a word with ancient origins, coming from the Old English *sael* and the Old French *salle*, both meaning a hall or spacious chamber. By the eighteenth century it referred to a large or lofty chamber serving as one of the principal reception rooms in a palace. Later, a salon was the reception room of a Parisian lady of fashion, and even later it came to mean a hall, usually in a public building, used for assemblies and entertainment, as in the American *saloon*. Salons have always seemed a little too exotic for ordinary houses in England and the United States.

Sitting room is a term dating only to the early nineteenth century. It refers to a room or apartment used primarily for sitting, alone or with company, distinct from the kitchen or bedroom. The sitting room was not usually the principal living room, and a grand house could have sitting rooms attached to each of the bedrooms.

Both the terms *living room* and *family room* came into use in the middle of the nineteenth century and meant essentially the same thing they do now: a room where the family carries on its ordinary activities. There was no real distinction between the two terms originally—*living* room did not imply a more formal space than *family* room—but they seem to have acquired slightly different shades of meaning as we use them today.

Whether you have a living room, family room, great room, or whatever, its purpose is simply to provide a congenial place for people to relax and enjoy one another's company. Here, I am using *living room* as a generic term, applicable to any indoor area that is primarily used for sitting and visiting, whether that space is formal or casual, separate or open to other parts of the home.

HOW TO DO IT Painted Sheer Curtains

You can easily add color to sheer curtains by painting them. I buy sheers from a discount department store, stretch them on a table or board, and paint them with artist inks. The inks come in many luminous colors and have no body, so they won't clog the holes in the curtains (but they are *not* washable). The paint will bleed through the sheer fabric, so you can't do designs that require much precision, but stripes, polka dots, and other simple patterns work fine.

ABOVE: *Use bold splashes of color to quickly update traditional rooms and furniture without detracting from their period charm.*

OPPOSITE: *A wood stove and a collection of plates displayed on a pine wall provide the backdrop for a conversation area in our guest house. The straight-back chair offers an alternative to couch seating for those who are just stopping by and don't want to settle in.*

Many people who have homes with both a living room and family room find that the more formal one is seldom used, even when they are entertaining guests. The reason is obvious: Most of the family's activities take place in the kitchen and the less-formal family room, and guests like to be where the action is. They don't feel comfortable in a room where they are excluded from the inner circle.

Until I moved into my present house, I never had more than one living area. In fact, I never had a living room that didn't share space with the kitchen, the dining room, or both. So I have always tried to create flexible social spaces capable of being cozy and casual or formally festive as the occasion requires.

We photographed quite a range of living rooms for this book in houses old and new. Some represent the type of traditional, separate living room or family room that is familiar to all of us. Others are less traditional spaces, including a sun porch that has been turned into a summer living room, and the sitting areas in a beachside summer house and a one-room guest house.

All of these spaces invite people to come in, sit down, and spend some time in conversation, reading, listening to music, or nodding off in a comfortable chair before the fire. Several common elements help to create that kind of space. First, it helps to have a variety of seating options, since not everyone prefers the same kind of chair and an individual's preferences might change with his or her mood or the situation.

For example, a person who intends just a short visit or is just passing through the room might perch on a simple straight-backed chair, but probably wouldn't settle into a sofa or an enveloping armchair.

People prefer chairs or sofas arranged in a conversational group around a focal point, such as a fireplace, a table, or a window, but they also like to be able to adjust the grouping by pulling up an additional seat or two when new people join the conversation. Having a few ottomans or lightweight chairs around the room enables them to do this. If the space if large enough, having several separate groups of chairs provides even more options.

Long winters require the kind of warmth and cheer found in this cozy red living room, with inviting chairs grouped around the glow of a fireplace.

HOW TO DO IT Painted Lamp Shade

Inexpensive lamp shades made of paper or fabric can be found in almost any discount department store or home center, and it takes only a little imagination and paint to turn a generic shade into a one-of-a-kind piece of decorative art. The shade pictured here is just fabric stretched over a wire form, available in any supply shop. It sits in the living room of a seaside cottage, and the design matches the painted upholstery on a nearby armchair.

If your shade is made of paper, you can paint it with artist inks, which leave the paper translucent so the colors glow when the lamp is lit. (Always use a low-wattage light bulb with a paper shade.) For a fabric shade, use fabric paint, which is more opaque. To create a colored background, simply buy a shade of that color.

Depending on the design you choose, you might want to paint freehand, use stencils, or draw the design on the shade with light pencil lines and then color it in. (Be careful not to make the pencil lines too dark, or they will show through when the lamp is lit.) When the design is dry, seal it with a clear finish, like artist gel medium or polyurethane.

The furniture in this seaside cottage living room is covered with hand-painted upholstery. The key to success with hand-painted fabrics is to use figures that are relatively large and simple. I painted these designs on plain canvas, which was then made into upholstery and treated to repel stains (see "How to Do It: Painted Fabrics" on page 109).

In my own living room (see overleaf), the walls are painted white to provide a simple gallery-like background for the many pictures displayed on them. I chose a white linen upholstery for a set of sofas and armchairs for the same reason: to set off the bright cushions and throws that provide splashes of color throughout the room. Several other chairs, ottomans, and benches are arranged around the room, creating additional pools of color with their rich plum and salmon upholsteries.

I don't think a living room should overwhelm people with color and pattern; the overall effect should be inviting and comfortable. But stimulating colors and patterns in rugs, upholstery, painted decorations, and ornaments will engage people's attention and interest, encouraging even shy or reticent visitors to be a little more outgoing. The room's decorations and furnishings will also give visitors who don't know you well a sense of who you are: your interests, your tastes, and maybe a bit of your history.

The ideal living room, I think, is one in which your family members feel perfectly at home and guests feel entirely welcome. I would like to think that a stranger left alone for a moment to wander around my living room would get the subliminal message: "This is who we are. Feel free to be yourself."

BELOW AND OPPOSITE:
A sun porch becomes a pleasant living room for the summer months. This one features a beautifully painted checkerboard floor (see "How to Do It: Painted Floors" on page 125). The seat of the bamboo couch has a vibrant yellow slipcover, and the scattered pillows pick up the greens and yellows of the garden.

LEFT: *In my own living room, a tall Swedish clock stands in the corner, next to a portrait painted by my great aunt Margarett Sargent.*

BELOW: *A few decorative details from my living room. Left to right: a cast-iron dog; a tassel on the ornate Swedish clock; the painted wooden chandelier suspended from the living room's cathedral ceiling.*

OPPOSITE: *Natural linen uphostery on my living room couches provides a neutral background for brightly colored pillows and other colorful accents, like the brilliant red ottoman. These accents can be changed seasonally, or whenever the mood to redecorate strikes.*

One of my more extravagant decorating projects. This built-in cupboard looks like a cross between a gypsy cart and a pagan temple. It was made from sections of a carved Indonesian cupboard that turned out to be too big to fit through any door of the house. Now it hides a television in our library/family room.

Laura Ashley

"HANDMADE PATCHWORKS, NEEDLEWORKS, RAG RUGS, LACE, AND WHITE STARCHED LINENS . . . ARE ALL BLISS TO ME. THESE THINGS TURN A LIVING ENVIRONMENT INTO A HOME."

Laura Ashley, 1925–1985

BELOW AND OPPOSITE: *Laura Ashley's fresh designs and quality fabrics brought a new spirit to interior decoration in the 1950s and '60s, reminding many people that do-it-yourself decorating was both practical and fun. (Photos courtesy of Laura Ashley.)*

People are sometimes surprised when I mention how much I admire Laura Ashley. "But your style is so different from hers!" they say. That's true, but not really relevant. She did good work as an artist, a craftsperson, and a businesswoman. She used high-quality, natural fabrics, created elegant designs in nice colors, and produced useful, well-made things.

The Laura Ashley style is so familiar today that it's hard to remember how fresh it was back in 1953, when she first began making silk-screen scarves on the kitchen table in her London apartment. Her original investment of ten pounds provided enough linen and dye for twenty scarves. She took them to the John Lewis store, which bought them and ordered more. Laura Ashley was in business.

Printing fabric and sewing scarves, table mats, and napkins were perfect at-home occupations for a young mother with an infant. But after a couple of years, Laura and her husband, Bernard, realized the business could be bigger than that. They moved the printing operation to a nearby basement, and Bernard quit his day job and went to work building more versatile dyeing and printing equipment.

Soon more products began to appear under the Laura Ashley name: dress fabrics, aprons, oven mitts, and gardening smocks. The Ashleys moved to a country cottage in Kent and set up a small factory in an old coach shed, expanding their production capabilities with better equipment and more help. But Laura still did all of the design work, finding inspiration in her garden and in textile designs of the eighteenth and nineteenth centuries.

In 1961 the Ashleys moved again, this time to Laura's native Wales, where they set up shop in Carno. Soon, with the help of ten employees, they were producing 5,500 yards of fabric per week. Then, in the mid-1960s, Laura created what came to be known as the Laura Ashley basic dress—a full-length, flowing cotton dress in muted colors. It could hardly have been more out of step with the fashion of the day, but it was an immediate hit.

When Laura Ashley died in 1985, her company employed four thousand people and owned eleven factories and 225 stores around the world. The product line had expanded to include furniture fabrics and wallpaper, and for many homeowners the Laura Ashley look—simple, pretty designs in strong, coordinated colors—represented the ideal in interior decoration.

In my opinion, Laura Ashley's greatest legacy was not the multinational business she created, nor the large archive of historical designs she collected and preserved. Her products inspired countless customers—ordinary people living in ordinary houses and apartments—to think about home decoration and to want high-quality materials. I suspect she actually raised the level of taste on two continents. How many artists have done as much?

Bedrooms

It is interesting that the form of a bed—a simple thing for a simple purpose—is so varied and culturally diverse. In the days before central heating or air conditioning, climate seemed to have much to do with bedroom styles. Old Scandinavian beds, like the ones in artist Carl Larsson's home, were built into the walls and hung with thick hand-woven curtains to keep the heat in on chilly Nordic nights. In India, simple beds with nets were better suited to survive the humidity and malarial mosquitoes. And when you walk through any historic palazzo or palace, you realize right away that the heroic, gilded grandeur of the bedroom was for public display, not personal comfort. (The breeze on a chilly night must have been horrific, even with the heavy hangings drawn.)

My English grandmother had a bedroom in London that was discreet and tasteful, with a goose-down quilt in soft pink, a pale-green silk chaise longue, a mirrored dressing table, and English floral curtains in good-quality fabric. It remained unchanged as long as she lived. My paternal grandfather, who lived for a long time in France, had a room with tall windows filled with light. It included a fireplace and not one, but two writing desks. It always seemed to me that being alone in one of those bedrooms was almost like being in my grandmother's or grandfather's presence. Everything in the room, from the incidental items on the bureau or dressing table to the way the pillows were arranged, suggested the character, personality, taste, and intellect of the occupant. That's not unusual, I know; we can always imagine our loved ones most clearly within the rooms that are or were most their own.

"I BELIEVE THAT EVERYTHING IN ONE'S HOUSE SHOULD BE COMFORTABLE, BUT ONE'S BEDROOM MUST BE MORE THAN COMFORTABLE: IT MUST BE INTIMATE, PERSONAL. . . . IT MAY BE AS SIMPLE AS A CONVENT CELL AND STILL HAVE THIS QUALITY OF THE PERSONALITY OF ITS OWNER."

Elsie de Wolfe, interior decorator, 1865–1950

LEFT: *This guest room is furnished with antique twin beds covered with woven linens and Swedish fabrics. A modern dhurrie rug lies on the painted floor between them.*

OPPOSITE: *The plank walls of this master bedroom are covered in lavender-blue distemper paint. The bed was made by Vermont craftsman Dan Mosheim, who fashioned its headboard with inlays of ebony and abalone.*

I have come across many amusing accounts of both well-known personalities and ordinary people who have conducted much of the business of their lives from their bedrooms. Disraeli handled affairs of state from his bed, and billionaire Armand Hammer was famous for directing his empire from his bedroom. Winston Churchill used to hold audience from both his bed and his bath. Nancy Mitford's social butterflies seem to spend their lives in bed, chatting on the phone, reading letters, entertaining visitors, and drinking tea or cocktails. My husband wrote ninety percent of his first five books in bed, and my idea of bliss is to be presented with a pot of tea in bed on a Sunday morning and to spend an extra hour reading before I face the world outside.

My own mother, with six children, used her bedroom as a burrow. She napped there, read there, and generally retreated there when we all became too much for her. The fireplace in her room was never lit except on Christmas morning, and the attached dressing room and bath were the hiding places for our Christmas presents each year. (We all knew it, pretended we didn't, and stealthily monitored the accumulation of gifts.) The beds in my mother's room had plain covers over electric blankets, and the carpet and curtains were quiet and dull. Yet the room was special and held its own familiar ceremonies and treasures.

One of those treasures was a box of old photos of the family: my mother, age three, in Regents Park on a pony; my parents on a ski holiday in Chile, looking young and stylish. Another treasure was my father's giant piggybank, which received his pocket change each night when he came home. Every few years, the pig became the prize in a family guessing game: How many pennies did it hold (winner take all)? My mother's jewelry box (she definitely was not a jewelry person) was always in a satisfying tangle, and every surface of her room was covered by an assortment of clumsy ashtrays, painted tiles, and artwork done at school by her young offspring.

The best thing about my mother's room was an attached screened sleeping porch. It had a bunk bed and our toy boxes and was our absolute favorite place to sleep on warm evenings. We built block castles and collected our stuffed animals there, staged battles and pillow fights, and had many a slumber party. Eventually the porch was glassed in and became a sun-filled sitting and writing room for my mother, whose obsession with gardening—at the time she was writing gardening advice for White Flower Farm—led to massive piles of garden catalogs towering in unsteady fashion all over the floor. If I were designing a house, I would definitely include a dressing room and a little work space off the bedroom.

Today's bedrooms seem to range from one extreme to the other. The master bedroom with dressing room and work space can be as vast and design-intensive as a small house. Or it can be a Zen-like, austere cell suitable for monks and quiet contemplation, free of any distraction. Or (and most familiarly) it can be a chaotic, multipurpose space—part dressing room, part laundry room, with dogs, craft projects, cribs, photo walls, computers, and libraries sharing the space.

ABOVE: *Think about arranging ordinary objects in unusual ways, such as propping a mirror on the floor against the wall rather than hanging it.*

OPPOSITE: *The mango-yellow paint on the walls of this room is one of my favorite bedroom colors (Benjamin Moore No. 153). I painted the rickety old bed in swirling shades of blue and gave a white lamp shade the same treatment (see "How to Do It: Painted Lamp Shade" on page 86).*

This bedroom does double duty as a bright, colorful living space. While the white walls and natural wood floor could hardly be simpler, a rainbow array of silk pillows lined up on the daybed fills the room with exuberant color. The rug, ceramics, and painted Swedish stool contribute additional color accents.

BELOW: *This guest room is painted in deep shades of rose, teal, and plum. Fireplaces and mantelpieces afford great opportunities to experiment with painting techniques.*

OPPOSITE: *I painted this beach cottage bedroom a glowing periwinkle blue, a color that always reminds me of the sea. The white upper walls, trim, and ceiling keep the room light and airy. High over the bed, a shelf holds summer icons, including beach stones, toy shovels, and fly swatters.*

The bed in a modern dressing room functions most of the time as a place to sort laundry, snuggle with small children, or pack a suitcase for the next business trip. Most of us have little time to be home at all, let alone dawdle in our bedrooms. Yet in our minds that room remains a place of comfort, rest, and solace, and we try to spend as much of our nonpublic lives there as possible. We love and live there, retreat there when we're sick, and—apartment or palazzo—consider it our own in ways that our other living spaces will never be.

I have always liked the thought of sleeping in a heroic bed that floated in the center of an enormous room like a ship. But such has not been my fate, and all of the bedrooms I have created in my life have been small, but multipurpose nonetheless. Certain features come before all other considerations: Bedrooms have to take advantage of views and light as much as possible. They need windows that open (in all types of weather, the wilder the better). They must have convenient places for stacks of in-progress reading. And the color of the room should look beautiful in any light, morning or night.

ABOVE: *After I painted this child's room, I decided that I didn't like the shade of blue, so I softened it by adding a cartoony outline of a bureau and a vase of flowers. I painted the design freehand, but the same could be done with stencils or by lightly laying down a design in pencil first.*

OPPOSITE: *This child's room is full of fun. The glossy-white painted bed and multicolored linens are set off by a checkerboard floor and striped walls. (See "How to Do It: Striped Walls" at right; for tips on painting a checkerboard floor, see "How to Do It: Painted Floors" on page 125.)*

Many people think that a small room must be white. I believe the reverse is true: A small room is an opportunity for color to glow. And the color choices for a bedroom are more varied and open to your taste than they might be in other, more public rooms. I know a woman whose bedroom is a saturated range of salmon pinks that look like lipstick. It's not my own taste, and I don't know how her husband—a guy's guy if there ever was one—feels about it, but it works for her, and that's all that matters.

I have painted bedrooms in every color from deep periwinkle blue to warm pumpkin yellow to lavender. I have painted baseboards, floor, and trim in colors that contrast with one another and with the wall color. I have also had a lot of fun painting freehand on walls with a light color over a strong one, working around the shape of the bedroom.

After the painting is done, we should never forget what a wonderful opportunity the bedroom offers for mercurial changes in color and pattern. Unlike slipcovers or rugs, bed linens can be found in a vast range of colors and designs at every price point. We can now "dress the bed" with as many different looks as we might find in our own wardrobes. Duvets (which have finally made their way into general acceptance in this country), mountains of pillows, bed skirts, and dust ruffles offer endless and extraordinary variety. You can change the look of your bedroom seasonally, just by changing the bed. Plain duvet covers can be bought at any chain department store and painted with user-friendly fabric paints for a special design. Kids can create their own bedding, even if they only have the stamina to do one pillowcase at a time.

HOW TO DO IT Striped Walls

I like striped walls for several reasons: They always seem to take people by surprise, they are inherently fun, and they let you use strong colors on the walls without having them become too overpowering. You can find a selection of colors and patterns in wallpaper, or work out your own colors and design for a painted wall.

The first two steps in painting a striped wall are the hardest: choosing the colors and the pattern. The simplest pattern is like the one shown here, two colors in stripes of equal width. But you could also add a third color or have wide stripes alternating with narrow ones. If you are particular, measure your walls and design a pattern that fits so you don't wind up with half a stripe at the corner.

To begin, cover the entire wall with two coats of either the lightest color

you're using or the most dominant one (the broadest stripe). When that color is dry, start at one corner and mark the position of each contrasting stripe with two pencil dots, one at the floor and the other at the ceiling. Connect the dots with removable painter's tape, aligning the tape with the outside edge of the stripe to be painted. (It's a good idea to draw arrows on each strip of tape to help you remember whether you'll be painting to the left of it or to the right.)

Paint the contrasting stripes. This will probably require two coats; possibly more if you are painting over a darker color.

Remove the painter's tape as soon as the paint is dry to the touch. The longer the tape stays on, the more likely it is to remove some of the paint when you peel it off.

HOW TO DO IT Painted Fabrics

Fabric paints are emulsion (water-based) paints that can be bought at most craft stores or on the Internet. Some of the paints have to be mixed with a fabric medium to help the fibers absorb and hold the color; others already include the medium. Once the paint dries, the color won't wash out.

You might want to start with pillowcases for your first experiment, or buy an inexpensive cotton sheet from a discount store. Be aware, however, that the quality of the fabric does affect the final result: The higher the material's thread count, the better it will turn out. Wash the fabric first to remove any sizing or other chemicals that might have been used to treat it.

I like large, bold designs for painted fabrics, but you can also paint extremely detailed figures. The design might be a pattern that repeats across the whole sheet, or you can arrange figures at random. If you don't trust your freehand painting skills, outline the figures lightly with tailor's chalk first. You can also use stencils, either purchased or cut yourself.

Stretch an old sheet across your work surface and staple it underneath like an ironing-board cover. (Hollow doors are my first choice for a craft table; they are cheap, lightweight, and can be found at any building supply store.) As you paint, keep the fabric you're working on stretched flat and pinned to the cover beneath it. Leave the fabric on the table until it's dry.

Some kind of heat treatment is usually necessary to make the color permanent—often it's as easy as going over the painted figures with a hot iron. The label on the paint container will tell you what to do.

LEFT: *The Blue Houses design on these duvet covers was one of my first for hand-painted fabric. I used a fat brush and a sponge to paint the figures. The lamp shade was made out of a piece of beaded chiffon with sequins.*

OPPOSITE: *This little guest room under the eaves has pale pink walls and an apricot floor. I call the design on the painted duvet cover Yellow Birds. The Bouquet rug is one of my most popular designs. (Photo by Didier Delmas.)*

The master bedroom in my first farmhouse has a wonderful fireplace and two-hundred-year-old doors. The bedcover is appliquéd cotton, an interpretation of early American folk art, in unusual colors of raisin, coral, and taupe. The lamp shades were painted with artist ink on parchment (see "How to Do It: Painted Lamp Shade" on page 86).

110

ABOVE: *When this photo was taken, my son's room was decorated for Christmas with appliquéd bedding in cheerful red and pillows with holiday designs. (Reprinted by permission, courtesy of Mary Engelbreit's Home Companion®. Photo by Gordon Beall. Copyright © 2000 Mary Engelbreit's Home Companion.)*

RIGHT: *Appliqué involves cutting out figures and stitching them onto a plain fabric background.*

OPPOSITE: *What could be more welcome on a cold wintry morning than breakfast in bed? The Yellow Bird ceramics complement the design on the bed linens. (Photo by Didier Delmas.)*

Armi Ratia and Marimekko

ABOVE: *Marimekko clothing from the 1960s was characterized by strong forms and colors.*

RIGHT: *One of Marimekko's signature designs: big, bold, amorphous flowers.*

OPPOSITE: *Some of Marimekko's classic fabric patterns. Clockwise from top left: Ostjakki, Unikko pink, Joonas, Unikko purple, Lokki red, Unikko yellow.*

When Marimekko fabrics first came to the United States in the late 1950s, nobody was quite sure what to make of them. The designs were big, bright, and bold—exuberant bursts of abstract art sold by the yard. Back in the Eisenhower era, cloth wasn't supposed to be that much fun. (Remember Mrs. Nixon's "good Republican cloth coat"? It was not a Marimekko design.)

Things changed in the early 1960s, when John F. Kennedy was in the White House and Jacqueline Kennedy was the most important trendsetter in the fashion world. She was photographed in several Marimekko dresses, and the Finnish label's U.S. sales soared. Suddenly, you saw Marimekko everywhere.

I remember going to the Design Research store in Boston to buy yards of Marimekko fabric when I was a high school student in the late 1960s. I used big pieces of the fabric for wall hangings in my room, as did many other girls at my school. When I went to my junior prom, it was in a brilliant orange Marimekko dress. I must have stood out like a flare. I don't remember the boy I went with, but I'll never forget that dress.

Marimekko was started in Helsinki, Finland, in 1951 by a visionary woman named Armi Ratia. Two years earlier, she and her husband, Viljo Ratia, had bought an old oilcloth factory with the intention of making printed fabrics under the company name Printex. They hired young designers straight out of school and gave them the freedom to try out their own ideas. The resulting printed cottons, strongly influenced by modern art trends, were often unconventional in both design and color combinations.

These extraordinary, brash fabrics did not catch on immediately. Clothing and home-furnishing manufacturers weren't accustomed to working with large patterns and bold colors and didn't quite know what to do with them. So Armi Ratia launched Marimekko to make a line of products demonstrating how the Printex textiles could be used. The new company's name came from a type of loose-fitting dress traditional in Finland and means, literally, "Mary's dress."

From the beginning, Marimekko ignored trends and conventional wisdom in both fashion and business management. The company's philosophy was to focus on making high-quality products with real artistic value while keeping the business as simple as possible. In the early years, all of the company's products were made by sewers working in their own homes, and when Marimekko had a show, it didn't use professional models, but had employees and friends wear the new designs instead. In spite of its unconventional attitude—or maybe because of it—the company's styles caught on in the European artistic community and then with the general public. They were first introduced in the United States by Design Research in 1959.

Armi Ratia died in 1979, and Marimekko has had its ups and downs since then, narrowly skirting bankruptcy and changing ownership twice. But some of the startling, beautiful fabrics that made the company a cultural phenomenon are still available, and it's remarkable how well those exuberant, in-your-face designs have held up. I loved them thirty years ago, and they still make me smile today.

Bathrooms

A builder once told me that renovating a bathroom is his favorite kind of job. It's a good thing he feels that way, because he works on a lot of them. Most builders do: Bathroom renovations are the second most common kind of remodeling job, after kitchen renovations. In 1999, Americans spent $2.5 billion upgrading their bathrooms.

The bathroom in the modern sense, equipped with a plumbed-in tub or shower and a flush toilet, is a relatively new idea, though public indoor bathing faciletes existed in some parts of the world as long ago as 2000 B.C., and some wealthy Romans had baths in their villas before the beginning of the Christian era. Practical flush toilets with wall-mounted cisterns existed in England by the 1870s, but they didn't become really common until near the turn of the twentieth century. It was the combination of the vitreous-china toilet, patented in England in 1875 by Thomas Twyford, and Thomas Crapper's design for a ball-and-siphon flushing system, patented in 1891, that eventually made the "water closet" a standard feature in almost every new home.

In the United States, few homes built before 1900 had bathrooms of any description. People used chamber pots (colloquially known as "thunder mugs") and outhouses instead of toilets, and bathing usually took place outside or in a washtub in the kitchen. Permanent bathtubs began to appear in upscale new houses about the middle of the nineteenth century, which is when the White House acquired one. Among the first entrepreneurs to recognize a potential market in bathroom fixtures was a manufacturer of farm equipment named John M. Kohler. He added legs to a combination horse trough and hog scalder, turning it into a tub.

Between 1900 and 1925, the bathroom became a standard feature in American homes. By 1920, building codes required them in new residential construction, and many people were quick to retrofit older houses as well. Even so, Census Bureau records show that as recently as 1950, more than one-third of the single-family houses in the United States did not have complete plumbing facilities (hot and cold piped water, a tub or shower, and a toilet).

Today, most people simply want more and more convenience and luxury in their bathrooms, and building-supply manufacturers keep finding ways to accommodate them. A master bathroom in a typical new house is likely to be equipped with two sinks, a tub, and a walk-in shower. It might also have a whirlpool, a bidet, and even a sauna. As each new luxury becomes widely available, it turns into a necessity, at least for the new-home market.

My own bathroom aspirations are less grand, and I have had bathrooms ranging from no-running-water-at-all in a vintage log house in Sweden (don't ask) to claw-foot tubs with ocean views. My bathroom-decorating philosophy has fortunately evolved from the truly eccentric style of my first decorating project. I was thirteen years old and had decided to paint my tiny bathroom. (One of the few advantages of growing up with four brothers was that I had my own bathroom, while they had to share.) My extremely tolerant mother agreed to my plan, as long as I did it myself, and she let me choose the colors.

"I READ ABOUT A WOMAN WITH TWENTY-ONE CHILDREN ONCE. THE BATHROOM WAS HER FAVORITE ROOM IN THE HOUSE. MINE, TOO."
Jane Smiley, writer, b. 1949

OPPOSITE: *Christine Miles painted a freehand design on her bathroom wall in shades of teal blue and created a gallery for her children's artwork. The rug is Thistle from my company's hooked rug collection.*

My ambitions were lofty, but I found my first painting job tedious. I kept myself going by changing colors for each wall: orange, lime, purple, pink, and black for the ceiling. (Think posters from Filmore East and you've got the general idea.) The effect was dramatic enough, but I quickly realized that drama is not what you want in a bathroom, a contemplative atmosphere being more appropriate. So not long after I completed the bathroom, I redid it, covering every inch of wall and ceiling with a collage of headlines and photos of pop stars clipped from magazines. For months afterward, soggy photos loosened by steam would drift down on me whenever I took a long bath.

My bathroom decorating has new parameters these days, and social consciousness and earthshaking colors are not among them. I leave all that at the door and simply look for comfort and peace once the door is closed and the world shut out. As far as I'm concerned, there are only a couple of necessities in a bathroom: a mix of soul-satisfying colors, a wonderful tub, and a great window. (If lack of privacy makes large windows a problem, glass block is an option, and skylights may be as well. There is nothing like gazing up at the cold winter stars when you are sunk to your chin in a hot bath.) I like bare floors of wood or tile, not carpeting, and I like to have the room to myself for long hot baths—as long as possible and as often as I can find the time.

BELOW RIGHT AND OPPO-SITE: *I painted the upper part of this bathroom's walls orange, then added a decorative pattern in cream and finished with a red glaze over all. The trim and half-height wainscoting is painted a glossy white to keep the room bright.*

BELOW LEFT: *An oddity of this old bathroom is a small arched window that looks through to the kitchen. This photograph was taken from the kitchen side.*

For many busy women, the bathroom is the ultimate retreat, the place we lurk when we need a break from the family, the phone, and our stressed-out lives. My English mother gave me a perfect model: the long soak in the tub with a good (not too heavy) book, door closed, and very hot water deep enough to hide under.

When I moved into my present house, a vintage farmhouse that had been remodeled somewhat in the 1960s, a new and improved bathroom was at the top of my list of priorities. The house had only one tub, short and rust-stained, tucked under the eaves in a little beige windowless room near an upstairs guest room. The downstairs bathroom, though remodeled, had only a shower. My husband's gift to me on our first anniversary was a bathroom of my own, with a wonderful, deep tub almost big enough for swimming laps.

ABOVE: *Natural art—summer meadow flowers in a vase made from a hollowed-out stone.*

OPPOSITE: *Just because a bathroom might be small doesn't mean you can't experiment with bold color choices. The walls of this guest bathroom are a mottled plum, which contrasts nicely against the blue-and-white tile splashguard. Stripped pine shutters can be closed across the tall window for privacy.*

HOW TO DO IT Painted Bathtub

Nothing beats an old claw-foot tub for a long, relaxing soak. Fixed up with a bright coat of paint and gleaming new faucets, it is a perfect blend of whimsy and practicality, the ideal centerpiece for any bathroom.

Painting an old bathtub isn't difficult but it can be messy, so make sure to protect the surrounding area carefully. First, remove any loose scale or rust from the exterior with a scraper, steel brush, and sandpaper. The surface must be clean, dry, and dust-free before you paint.

Prime the surface with a rust-inhibiting metal primer, and, when the primer has dried, apply several coats of glossy enamel paint in the color of your choice. It's best to apply a number of thin coats to avoid drips or sags. Leave the tub a solid color or add surface decoration with stencils or freehand designs.

I painted the bathroom to remind me of my beloved ocean: white bead-board walls with details painted in shades of blue-green and a frieze of soft violet-blue at the top. All of those colors are combined in a backsplash of hand-painted ceramic tiles running the length of the wall behind the tub. The tub is built into a bead-board enclosure, with a ledge all around for books, a glass of wine, a candle, or a handful of stones or shells from the last trip to the sea. I painted the floor in a freehand checkerboard of soft periwinkle and white, and in the summer baptisia plants in the same blue crowd the window from the garden outside. After a long day I flee to this room, where I can have a long soak, stare foolishly at nothing, and shed the cares of the day. It's perfect.

ABOVE: *The mirror in my bathroom came from an antique dresser. The old glass is blue-tinged and wavy, adding to the aquatic impression I wanted to create in the room.*

OPPOSITE: *My bathroom is full of watery colors, from the painted tiles behind the tub to the pattern on the floor and towels stacked on a convenient chair. The band of blue above the bead board sets off pitchers displayed on a high shelf.*

HOW TO DO IT Painted Floors

In my first farmhouse, the floors in the four upstairs bedrooms were each painted a different color: glossy white, apricot, pale green, and lavender. I found the change in colors beautiful as I walked from room to room. My present house also has a number of painted floors, but my favorite is the periwinkle-and-white checkerboard pattern in the bathroom.

PREPARATION

Make sure the floorboards are securely nailed down, with no protruding nail heads. Serious cracks or holes can be filled with wood putty, but don't worry about every little dent or knothole. Scrape and sand the floor just enough to remove loose paint and provide a reasonably smooth surface. Vacuum the floor, scrub it with water and a detergent like TSP (trisodium phosphate), rinse, and allow it to dry thoroughly.

Two coats of primer will smooth the surface and provide a good foundation. If the floor will be painted a dark color, use a dark-toned primer.

PAINTING A SOLID COLOR

Once the floor is primed, use a glossy enamel, like the porch-and-deck enamels made by major paint manufacturers. Most places will mix any color for you, just as they would for wall paint. Use two coats of the color to avoid skips and uneven shading.

PAINTING A CHECKERBOARD PATTERN

If you'd like to get more decorative, the easiest pattern to paint on your floor is that old standard, the checkerboard, made up of light- and dark-colored squares laid out diagonally. The scale of the square blocks can be altered to suit any room. Decide how large you think the blocks should be, then cut a piece of cardboard that size and lay it on the floor to see how it looks.

Use the cardboard square to draw outlines for the blocks with a pencil on the primed white-base floor. Start with a block at the very center of the floor, then work out from that point. Some people like to chart the pattern out on graph paper to avoid incomplete blocks at the edges; you can also cheat by stopping when you've finished the last row that fits completely, then painting a solid-colored border around the whole room in either the same or a contrasting color.

I paint the blocks freehand, as I like the slightly irregular effect this gives, but you can use removable painter's tape to outline every other block if you want clean, straight lines. Paint all of the light blocks first, giving them two coats. Once the paint is dry, move the tape to the inside edges of the light blocks and paint the darker ones. You can also embellish the checkerboard pattern with designs in each colored block.

Allow each coat of paint to dry thoroughly. For the best possible finish, sand very lightly and vacuum between coats. When completely dry, cover the floor with several coats of polyurethane.

While some people's tastes may run to glittering marble or chrome and yards of thick pile carpet, the best bathroom I ever saw was on Roque Island in Maine, for more than a century the property of the Gardner family (of Isabella Stewart Gardner fame). The huge, one-hundred-year-old summerhouse still has no electricity, and one of the original bathrooms has a fireplace, a faded stenciled floor, an enormous free-standing tub, kerosene lamps, and a perfect window looking out at the sea. This is not just a bathroom; it is a fantasy place, combining all the most primal elements: air, light, water, fire. It is marvelous and timeless.

Unless it is really enormous, a bathroom offers opportunities for many bite-size decorating projects that can be done in a weekend. Painting the floor or the walls, trimming a wood-framed mirror, or making tiles at a paint-it-yourself pottery places—these are all projects that will make your bathroom a truly personal space. One of my favorite projects is painting an old claw-footed tub. If you use a bright enamel on the outside, with stenciled or freehand designs, the tub will look antique and modern at the same time (see "How to Do It: Painted Bathtub" on page 122).

The bathroom is a great place to decorate, because you don't have to take it at all seriously. (If you do start to take it seriously, just picture yourself in the tub.) Choose any colors you like; hang up artwork or photographs; display small collections of ceramics or glass, a vase of fresh flowers, or beach treasures laid on the window ledge. Or paint the whole room white and keep it as quiet, plain, and simple as a cell. This is fundamentally a private room; there's no one to please but yourself and no reason not to make it exactly the way you want it.

HOW TO DO IT Collage Mirror

This bathroom mirror started out as a very ordinary item: just a simple wall mirror in a wood frame—a junk store item, basically. We needed a mirror for the bathroom in our company office, so I just painted the frame with some chrome-yellow paint I had sitting around and a freehand design. Still, it just sort of hung on the wall without saying anything. It wasn't good company.

A short while later, I came across some wooden figures in my studio—farm animals and stars that had been used as Christmas ornaments—and glued a few of those to the mirror frame. It started to perk up. I added some sequins, wood and glass beads, a toy truck, and a couple of small ceramic knobs—it was pretty much a direct transfer from my junk drawer to the mirror frame.

You'd be amazed how many enthusiastic comments this mirror has prompted from visitors—not because it's elegant or beautiful or even well made, but just because it's quirky and fun!

The Omega Workshops and Charleston

Vanessa Bell's bathroom at Charleston. The panel was painted by Duncan Grant in 1945; the hanging cupboard by Angelica, Duncan and Vanessa's daughter, in the late 1930s. The portrait of Angelica's daughter, Nerissa, was painted by Duncan in 1965. (Photo © Alan MacWeeney from Charleston, A Bloomsbury House & Garden.*)*

If, as the old spiritual says, there is a mansion awaiting each of us in heaven, I hope mine will be decorated by the artists of the Omega Workshops. A couple of dozen artists worked for Omega at one time or another during its brief existence (1913–1919). By agreement, they never signed the pieces they created, but almost all of their work—furniture, carpets, curtains, clothing, ceramics, wallpapers, toys, and a host of other everyday items—was imaginatively designed, brilliantly colored, and executed with enthusiastic spontaneity.

Roger Fry was the driving force behind Omega. A former curator of the Department of Paintings at the Metropolitan Museum of Art in New York, he was a highly regarded art historian and critic. When he fell out with the British art establishment over his enthusiasm for the new Post-Impressionist art of France, he became a kind of hero to many young British artists. He conceived of Omega as a way to provide financial support for those artists: If they couldn't earn a living selling their paintings or sculpture, they could practice their art as decorators and perhaps elevate the nation's taste in the process. "I hope I may be able to pull it [the Omega Workshops] through," Fry wrote in a letter. "If I do I shall, I think, have done something to make art possible in England. It would be of course almost to accomplish a miracle, but I have hopes."[1]

Joining Fry as co-directors of Omega were artists Vanessa Bell and Duncan Grant. Like Fry, Bell and Grant were central figures in the amazing circle of writers, artists, and intellectuals known as the Bloomsbury Group. They shared Fry's interest in Post-Impressionism, and their work set the style for the "Bloomsbury interior." Bell and Grant devoted much of their time and attention to Omega, creating many of its most memorable pieces, until 1916, when they moved from London to Charleston, a rambling farmhouse in the heart of the Sussex downs.

From the beginning, the Omega Workshops were an artistic success, and at first the business didn't do badly financially, either. A writer for *The Times* of London, reporting on the opening of the Omega showrooms in London's Bloomsbury district, observed: "What pleases us most about all the work of these artists is its gaiety. They seemed to have worked, not sadly or conscientiously upon some artistic principle, but because they enjoyed doing so."[2] There were many customers, although the best ones were always friends of the artists. But with the beginning of World War I in 1915, many of the young artists were called up for military service, and avant-garde home furnishings dropped off the must-have list for just about everyone in England. By 1919, Fry had tired of the

demands the business placed on him. He liquidated Omega and took off to paint in France and explore the possibility of starting an artists' colony on the Mediterranean.

Since all of the items made by Omega were intended for daily use rather than display, few have survived more than fourscore years of wear and tear. Many were destroyed by attacks on London during the two world wars. The best place to see surviving examples and to get a sense of the spirit behind Omega is at Charleston, which Bell and Grant kept as a summer home throughout their lives. (Bell died in 1961, Grant in 1978.) Its rooms reflect sixty years of artistic creativity—murals, painted furniture, ceramics, paintings, and textiles. Visiting Charleston, one can easily picture Bell as she was described by her sister, Virginia Woolf, in 1919: "painting all the time, 'til every inch of the house is a different colour."[3]

Charleston is, in fact, the most extraordinary masterpiece left behind by the two principal Bloomsbury artists. "There is a wonderfully uninhibited, irreverent quality to the decoration of the house which is that

of a child let loose to experiment," wrote Virginia Nicholson, Bell's granddaughter. "Part of the exhilaration that people experience from looking at the brilliantly colourful designs that crowd the Charleston walls and furniture comes from that sense of confidence and fearlessness."[4]

Charleston is now maintained by the Charleston Trust and is open to the public five afternoons a week from May through October. The house and furnishings have been carefully restored to the way they were when Bell and Grant lived there. Walking through the rooms, one almost feels that the artists have just stepped out to the garden for a moment. I'd be willing to wait a long, long time if I really thought they might come back.

....

[1] *Omega and After: Bloomsbury and the Decorative Arts,* by Isabelle Anscombe. London: Thames and Hudson, 1981, pp. 25–26.
[2] *Bloomsbury Portraits,* by Richard Shone. London: Phaidon Press Ltd., 1993, p. 103.
[3] *Omega and After,* p. 103.
[4] *Charleston: A Bloomsbury House & Garden,* by Quentin Bell and Virginia Nicholson. London: Frances Lincoln Ltd., 1997, pp. 6–7.

A view of what was called the green bathroom. The bathtub was painted by Richard Stone, a friend of Duncan's, in 1970. The picture above the bath is Apples, *painted by Duncan around 1935–1940. (Photo © Alan MacWeeney from* Charleston, A Bloomsbury House & Garden.*)*

Outdoor
Spaces

For me, the first sign of approaching spring is when I begin to hear owls calling from the woods beyond the pond. This happens in mid-February, often on some of the coldest nights of the winter, long before the robins return or we hear the clamor of the wild geese coursing overhead or the spring peepers in the pond below the house. It means that the days are lengthening and warming. Within a week or two, we'll see our neighbors out hanging their buckets or checking the pipelines that will collect the flowing maple sap. Then the temperature will begin climbing above freezing during the day, the snow will start to slump, and we'll slide into that strange in-between time that New Englanders call "mud season."

It's barred owls that we hear most often—"eight-hooters" they're called, because of their twice-repeated four-note refrain: "hoohoo hoo-hoo," "Who cooks for you?" I lie awake for awhile, cozy under the blankets, listening to owl song. And even though the temperature outside might be so cold I can hear the trees snap and pop, my mind will turn with eager—and premature—anticipation to thoughts of a new season: What will we do with the flower borders this spring? Does the porch furniture need repainting? Where did we put the hammock? How soon can the lettuce seeds go in? Even when we still need a fleece jacket or sweater, those of us who live in northern climates expect to spend every conceivable moment, April through October, living outside.

So eager are we to start tracking the spring that we start moving activities outdoors as soon as we get a few consecutive days with temperatures in the forties. I move one or two of our wicker armchairs from the barn to the south-facing porch, along with a small table for teacups. Soon the daffodils are up, and there are days warm enough to eat lunch outside, so more chairs and a larger table come out of hibernation and settle on the terrace looking out on the mountains. By the time the lilacs are blooming and daylight stretches long into the evening, our living room has vanished from our minds, and we sit, read, and eat on the porch and stone terrace. When I'm working at home, I take the cordless phone and my laptop and set myself up on the porch.

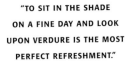

"TO SIT IN THE SHADE ON A FINE DAY AND LOOK UPON VERDURE IS THE MOST PERFECT REFRESHMENT."
Jane Austen, novelist, 1775–1817

LEFT: *Old chairs in mixed colors stand ready for any passerby who wants to stop for awhile to view the progress of the garden.*

OPPOSITE: *The bead-board ceiling of our front porch is painted a light blue and the floor is green-gray—cool, restful colors for a hot, bright day. We practically live here and on the adjacent terrace during the summer months.*

This little screen house overlooks our swimming pond—the one the geese don't use. Occasionally I can escape up here for a midday nap or a good read, and it's perfect for dreaming, whether awake or asleep. A couple pieces of sheer fabric hung from the ceiling blow gently in the wind, and an assortment of simple silk ornaments decorated with beads and ribbons sway back and forth on long cotton threads.

By the time real summer weather arrives, we've basically moved out of the house altogether, often spending the night in the old sugar house a short walk up the hill. We converted the sugar house into a guest cottage several years ago, never anticipating how much time we would spend there ourselves. It has its own pond, larger and deeper than the one by the farmhouse, and we go up there to swim, watch the sky, and feel the wind. A small screen house across the pond from the sugar house serves on occasion for a secluded afternoon nap or for relief from the few hot nights we get in Vermont.

Even our boys are infected by the madness and alternate between sleeping in a three-story tree house that they built the summer before last and in hammocks strung from trees. Traveling in a pack as they do, these Vermont teenagers seem to barely come indoors at all, spending virtually all their time outside, working, swimming, biking, socializing, kicking balls around, or grilling.

An outdoor room can be anything from a porch or terrace to an enclosed structure with a roof, like our screen house. It might also be just a corner of the yard or garden, defined by a flagstone terrace or flower borders. In fact, you don't need to define the boundaries at all. Place a few chairs beneath a favorite tree or a picnic table on the lawn, and they will claim the space around them for your outdoor room.

BELOW: *Outdoor furniture winds up wherever we might want to use it—in this case, outside an old farm shed at the Grover farm. Reading in the sun is always more inviting than mowing the lawn or hoeing weeds.*

OPPOSITE: *We cleared out the same shed shown below to give visiting children their very own guest house. Here, hand-painted sheets and cozy pillows make the place homey and comfortable for Emma and Wally.*

Our outdoor furniture is an eclectic mix of old wicker, flea-market tables, long folding lawn chairs, and garden-catalog teak. All of the wooden pieces are painted, both for fun and to protect them from the weather. Over the years I have painted the assorted wooden chairs and benches that are scattered over our terrace in a range of blues, whites, and teal greens that work well with our landscape. Some of the small flea-market side tables have gotten more elaborate touches of paint and surface pattern, as have a set of outdoor rustic chairs at our beach cottage.

HOW TO DO IT Painted Outdoor Furniture

Most of my outdoor furniture is painted with exterior latex enamel in mix-and-match colors—sometimes several colors on a single piece. Since individual pieces tend to migrate over the course of the summer, I never know which colors might wind up together.

Refinishing a piece of outdoor furniture should begin with a good cleaning and inspection. Tighten any loose fasteners and replace missing or broken hardware. Remove loose or blistering paint with a scraper or sandpaper, and wash off any dirt, grease, or oil.

If the old paint is in very bad shape and has to be sanded down to bare wood in places, start with a coat of exterior primer. You should also put one or two coats of primer on any new, unfinished pieces of furniture. If the finish coat will be a dark color, use primer that has been tinted to make an approximate match.

If you are just touching up a previously painted piece using the original color, a single coat should be enough. A dramatic change in color might require several coats. Decorative patterns can be added after the base color has thoroughly dried.

ABOVE AND LEFT: *I painted these cedar chairs at our beach house in colors suggesting the sea and then decorated them with wavy patterns.*

OPPOSITE: *The stone terrace outside our kitchen is the most popular gathering place for friends and family on long summer evenings. The peonies were plucked from a border beside the porch just a few feet away.*

Being able to entertain guests outside is one of the very best things about summer. It doesn't get much better than eating under the stars, surrounded by blinking fireflies and the scent of flowers. What entertaining we do, we tend to plan for summer, to take advantage of the lovely landscape we live in and avoid setting up our guests for icy winter travel to our remote farm. Any location on our farm can become the outdoor room of the day, and we define "living room" or "dining room" simply by where we place the furniture and food on that occasion.

Our most ambitious outdoor party brought about seventy friends to the farm on a beautiful summer evening, and the outdoor room was a fifty-acre hilltop field. We gambled on the weather, planning to use our big hay barn as a backup, and a day of worrisome thunderstorms gave way just in time to a beautiful late-August evening. Our party began with wine and hors d'oeuvres on the lawn by the pond next to the house. At dusk, we walked up through the fields to one of our upper pastures, where we had set up sawhorses and boards to make one long table, decked out with tablecloths, candles, and abundant flowers from our garden and fields. From the middle of that hayfield no other lights can be seen, and we were ringed by mountains, topped by stars. A friend and caterer, accustomed to preparing gourmet dinners and fancy weddings, managed brilliantly without electricity, cooking on grills and keeping hot dishes warm over gas burners. Wine and desserts were packed in ice-filled coolers.

Our party that night was in the tradition of what people do in Sweden, where the winters are even darker and longer than ours in New England. We lived for *Midsommar* on June 21, when music, flowers, food, and wine celebrated the coming of the long days. Everyone stays outside throughout the night in a true celebration, in tune with the season. While our guests reluctantly went home before dawn, we will never forget the grand dining room that sprang to life in a hayfield that night.

ABOVE: *Wrought-iron furniture in a favorite corner of the garden instantly defines its own outdoor room.*

LEFT : *Pillows and pots of flowers add color to this terrace at a friend's house. She painted her benches, chairs, and tables to match in glossy white.*

OPPOSITE: *A table by the pond is an idyllic setting for supper, with a bright tablecloth and a vase of peonies contributing just the right touch of elegance. For obvious reasons, we seldom dine indoors in the summer.*

Summer is indeed too short, and when the leaves are falling and the geese are gone, we store most of the outdoor furniture away, always leaving a few chairs on the porch for warm autumn afternoons. Then we're restricted to indoor living again, happy enough to be inside when snow swirls across the porch and collects in drifts against the terrace's stone walls. During that long season we'll have morning tea and coffee by the window, looking at the patterns of the skeletal trees against the white fields, and we'll have dinners at the table in front of the fire. It's a great time for projects, for painting things, or redecorating as our focus turns back to the inside of our homes.

Summer is just long enough that we are ready for those cool nights to return, for the light to change, for the realization that we'd better settle back down to real work. At night we'll sleep warm under heavy comforters, listening to the wind rattling ice in the branches of the trees outside, with its own kind of charm. But I'm dreaming of that day when we open all the windows to the breezes and move our daily lives back outside. I'm waiting to catch the first haunting notes of owl song.

Pulling It All Together: The Grover Farm

A few months before I began writing this book, my husband, Tom, and I bought the farm that bordered our own on the west. With it came a large dairy barn, a number of tractor sheds, and other outbuildings. The original house dates to the late 1700s, but it was expanded in 1840 with the addition of a wing that was really a whole new Federal-style farmhouse. We bought it after the last family member to live there died at the age of 103. Hazel Grover, born at the farm, had lived there alone for many years, leasing the barns and pastures to a dairy farmer.

We didn't need or want more land and buildings, particularly buildings in such sad disrepair as those on the Grover farm. Our own farm has more than enough land on a beautiful hillside, with an old farmhouse that we have renovated extensively. Tom has a separate building for his office, and we have plenty of room for our two boys when they're home. Our barn and pastures are more than adequate for our menagerie—some fifty sheep, five goats, two alpacas, one horse, an indeterminate number of chickens and geese, and three very noisy donkeys—and there are woods and fields enough for a lifetime of rambling explorations with the dogs. (If it sounds like heaven, it is.)

Still, when we heard that the Grover farm was for sale, we had to look into it. We live in the Mettowee Valley, one of the relatively few parts of Vermont where farming is still a feasible way to make a living, and we have long been active in efforts to preserve this area's agricultural heritage and landscape. We didn't want to see another working farm turn into building lots.

Besides, the house on the Grover farm is the only one you can actually see from our own. At night, the lighted windows of the two houses wink at each other across a half-mile of fields, a little wooded swale with a creek running through it, and a winding two-lane road. So when we bought it, the farmhouse was already like an old friend.

Our original idea was to buy the farm, hold onto a piece that bordered our land on two sides, and sell everything else, including the house and other buildings, to the Vermont Land Trust. The trust could then resell the property to a farmer, with deed restrictions protecting it from development.

That was the plan, but that's not how it turned out. As soon as we owned the place, we fell in love with the old house, unimproved and weather-beaten as it was, and we decided to keep it. We extended the lease on the land and barn to a neighboring dairy farmer who has been using them for twenty years, and we're still putting a conservation restriction on the deed to preserve the farmland in perpetuity.

Keeping the Grover farm meant it was time to rearrange my work life. I had been doing most of my design work in a studio that was a fifteen-minute drive from home. Commuting fifteen minutes through the Vermont countryside is hardly a hardship, even when half the distance is on dirt roads that turn into sloughs during mud season and sheets of ice on bitter winter days. But commuting ten minutes on foot through our own fields is even better. My studio staff was growing, and we had already talked about the need to move to bigger quarters. In short, we decided to relocate my studio to the Grover farmhouse.

"IT IS ALL VERY WELL TO PLAN OUR IDEAL HOUSE OR APARTMENT, OUR INDIVIDUAL CASTLE IN SPAIN, BUT IT ISN'T NECESSARY TO LIVE AMONG INTOLERABLE FURNISHINGS JUST BECAUSE WE CANNOT REALIZE OUR CASTLE. THERE NEVER WAS A HOUSE SO BAD THAT IT COULDN'T BE MADE OVER INTO SOMETHING WORTHWHILE. WE SHALL ALL BE VERY MUCH HAPPIER WHEN WE LEARN TO TRANSFORM THE THINGS WE HAVE INTO SOME SEMBLANCE OF OUR IDEAL."

Elsie de Wolfe, interior decorator, 1865–1950

OPPOSITE: *The entry hall at the Grover farmhouse is painted in shades of blue and flooded with light through windows on two sides. The open door affords a glimpse of the dining room.*

The farmhouse is not very large and is in two sections. The old end was in abysmal shape when we bought it: plaster and lath falling down, no insulation, no water or bathroom, terrifying wiring, and only a wood stove for heat. That section became the new studio, on two floors. The 1840 addition was in somewhat better condition. We did a minimally invasive restoration in this part of the house, turning it into a showcase for my company's products and designs. It also serves as a guest house for visiting family and friends.

Renovating the house was a six-month project, with me as general contractor and a team of builders led by Paul Roberts doing almost all of the work. We wanted to keep the changes in the main part of the house as unobtrusive as possible. A few structural repairs were required, and the builders replaced the ancient wiring and plumbing, patched and painted the plaster, and refinished the original floors.

There are eight rooms in that main part of the house: an entry hall, parlor, dining room, bathroom, and tiny kitchen downstairs, and three small bedrooms upstairs. For me, the most exciting part of the renovation was decorating all of those rooms at the same time, starting with a blank slate. Every color, every bit of decoration, every piece of furniture could be chosen for its contribution to the overall effect. The number of decisions to be made could have been overwhelming, if each one wasn't so much fun.

BELOW: *Distemper softens the color of the lime-green walls in the living room. The fireplace surround is purely ornamental; it came from another house.*

OPPOSITE: *I assembled a riotous array of fabric colors in the living room, but they work—loudly—with the green walls. The floor was originally painted but was sanded down to bare wood.*

Paint is a miraculous tool for giving furniture new life. These two pieces—a new, unfinished table and an old cabinet—were easily transformed for the dining room at the Grover farm. For the table I chose a bold chrome yellow for the pedestal base and a quiet blend of several grays and white for the patterned top. For the cabinet I went with a more colorful mix of blues and grays.

PREPARATION

If you're working with an old piece of furniture, wash off any dirt and grime, scrape off loose paint or varnish, and sand the rough spots. It's not necessary to remove every trace of an old finish.

If you are working on an unfinished piece with knots or streaks, prime it with at least two coats of sealer. New wood should also be primed. (I always start with a coat of primer, even on previously painted pieces, as it provides a smooth surface for the base coat.) Water-based acrylic primer is easy to use, dries quickly, and cleans up with soap and water.

PAINTING

Decide on the colors and pattern for your project. If the piece will have a regular pattern, like the white triangles around the edge of my table, mark the pattern on the primer and use a different base color for that part, as it is difficult to paint light colors over dark. You will need two or three coats to get even shading throughout. I prefer a satin-finish water-based paint; if you want a shiny finish, it's best to add that later with a coat of polyurethane.

When painting a surface pattern on top of a base coat, work with one color at a time and start with the bigger shapes, so you can balance the colors and pattern across the piece. You should have an idea of what the design will look like, but don't think too hard! If you do something you don't like, you can wipe the mistake away with a damp sponge or paint over it later. For my tabletop, I just added some swirling patterns to the gray base, using three lighter shades of gray, until I achieved an effect that I liked.

FINISHING

Furniture, particularly tables and chairs, gets a lot of wear, so the paint needs to be protected by a hard finish. I used glazing liquid to finish my tabletop because I like the soft luster it gives to paint. Polyurethane (available in glossy, eggshell, or matte finishes) provides better protection. Apply two or three coats, following the manufacturer's instructions.

In the dining room, I painted a chunky armoire in shades of blue and gray to create a rustic marble effect. The base of the painted table is chrome yellow with a distemper glaze, while the top is patterned with several shades of gray.

Since the house was to be a showplace for my company's home furnishings, I needed to decorate it in colors that would set off my own palette. The old-fashioned layout of the ground floor provided an intriguing opportunity to experiment with different combinations of colors for walls and floors. The rooms open into one another with few doors—wherever you are, you can see into at least two other rooms, and from some points of view, you can see into five other rooms. So the colors in any given room had to work in combination with those in all of the connecting rooms.

RIGHT: *This is a view of the dining room through the kitchen door. The kitchen wainscoting is painted olive green, while the walls above are pale sage.*

OPPOSITE: *The colored tiles above the counter in the kitchen were custom painted (see "How to Do It: Painted Ceramic Tiles" below). The stove is a restored O'Keefe and Meritt from the 1940s.*

HOW TO DO IT Painted Ceramic Tiles

Painted tiles are a great way to add some distinctive and personal decoration to a kitchen or bathroom. If you intend the tiles for display only, and don't mean to actually use them, they won't even need to be fired in a kiln. Just buy some blank tiles from a craft-supply store or a mail-order company, paint them, and, when they're dry, apply a coat of varnish to protect them.

   If you prefer to fire the tiles, visit a local ceramics workshop—most cities have one. There you'll have access to materials, tools, and coaching. I've used painted tiles in every home I've owned, though they have never been my own work. The tiles shown here were painted by Vermont potter Jane Davies.

For the walls I chose distemper paint, which can be made up in strong colors but has good pigments and creates a kind of a hazy effect that softens the tones. I used lime green in the living room, an orangey coral in the bathroom, soft pale green in the kitchen, dove gray in the dining room, and soft blue-green in the hall.

Upstairs, I did one bedroom in mango yellow, one in vivid cobalt blue, and the third in a light blue covered with simple hand-painted patterns. I used three different shades of blue-green to blue-lavender in the upstairs and downstairs halls, and painted the floors in two of the bedrooms, one white and the other pale green.

Seen in combination, these colors are definitely bright and cheerful, but not overwhelming. The effect is like looking at an early-spring landscape under a clear sky: blues and greens blending into an overall theme. To furnish the house, I chose rugs, cushions, fabrics, and painted furniture with splashes of bright fruit colors: blueberry, orange, lemon, cherry, and grape.

While it is unusual to see so much color in such a traditional old house, I really like the way it turned out. When we bought it, the house was sad and tired and down at the heels, a piece of the past with no part in the future. We kept faith with the past, leaving the many wonderful old features intact, but brought the building back to life with new color, new purpose, and lots of plans. It was the least we could do for a neighbor.

This bureau was chipped and charmless, but it had an unusual shape, and a coat of green paint put it to rights. The walls of this bedroom are distempered blue; other shades of blue can be seen in the hallway beyond the door.

ABOVE: *A single bed in the blue bedroom is made up with an antique quilt and coral pillows. The open door leads to an adjoining bedroom.*

LEFT: *These plaster walls were in rough shape. I quickly patched and painted them with a one-color pattern to hide the worst flaws. A rose-colored sari covers a doorless closet.*